WALNUT CREEK

W C Apr 1992

I0949521

WITHDRAWN

PRACTICAL TRAINING
FOR BIG DOGS

PRACTICAL TRAINING
FOR
BIG DOGS

Lesley Bygrave
and Paul Dodd

Contra Costa County Library

APR 01 1992

HOWELL BOOK HOUSE
New York

3 1901 01676 7099

Copyright © 1989 by Howell Book House

Photographs Peter Hobson
Illustrations Maggie Stovold
© Lesley Bygrave & Paul Dodd 1989

All rights reserved. No part of this book may be reproduced or transmitted in any form or by any means, electronic or mechanical, including photocopying, recording or by any information storage and retrieval system, without permission in writing from the Publisher.

HOWELL BOOK HOUSE
Macmillan Publishing Company
866 Third Avenue, New York, NY 10022
Collier Macmillan Canada, Inc.

First printing 1989

Library of Congress Cataloging-in-Publication Data

Bygrave, Lesley,
    Practical training for big dogs / Lesley Bygrave & Paul Dodd [photographs. Peter Hobson : illustrations, Maggie Stovold].
        p. cm.
    Includes index.
    ISBN 0-87605-771-7
    1. Dogs—Training   I. Title   II. Title: Big dogs.
SF431.D635   1989   89-33951
636.7'088'7—dc20   CIP

Macmillan books are available at special discounts for bulk purchases for sales promotions, premiums, fund-raising, or educational use. For details, contact:
                    Special Sales Director
                    Macmillan Publishing Company
                    866 Third Avenue
                    New York, NY 10022

10 9 8 7 6 5 4 3 2

Printed in Great Britain

Contents

Dedicated to Thor

Metropolitan Police Dog Monroes Thor U.D. Ex. W.D. Ex. P.D. Ex

Introduction

Some of the techniques for training and handling a big dog are different to those needed with small breeds. The differences are most usually seen in the home as they result from the sheer size of the animal and the need to have him, therefore, under tight control. A badly behaved Yorkshire Terrier can be lifted up and shaken; also he is unlikely to cause massive damage or stand on a stool to steal meat from the kitchen worktops. A badly behaved Great Dane cannot be lifted – even as a 6-month puppy he is very heavy – and he can take anything he wishes from the kitchen worktop without even stretching. A big dog can cause havoc in a home in terms of damage to property and, in some instances, people. Friends will often tolerate a visiting Pekinese that jumps on the sofa or puts his paws on people's legs, but they feel very differently when a large Bull Mastiff decides to make a bed on their best furniture.

A big dog, unlike a smaller brother, cannot be trained by strength alone; it is stupid to try. And a big dog that is not under voice and lead control can use brute strength at any point to pull away from the owner and create an accident.

This book will tell you all you need to know about basic training for a big dog, be he pedigree, crossbreed, puppy or adult. What it will not do is make time for you to do the training, nor will it teach you the patience you will need to cultivate unless you are already a patient person. Time, patience, firmness and consistency are all crucial elements in dog training. A few occasional lessons are useless as the dog cannot be expected to remember a couple of hours' training; he needs constant reinforcement of the words and responses. Lack of time is no excuse. A person who maintains he cannot beg or steal at least half an hour a day for a few months to train his dog, should not own one.

With dog training, patience becomes a necessity, not a virtue. How frustrating it is when a dog is learning well and suddenly, one evening during training, he forgets everything and dashes deafly across the park to mug another dog. If you aren't to throw away all your hard work, you just take a deep breath and patiently press on, reminding him again what behaviour you do and do not expect of him.

Above all, you have to learn to overcome that very English tendency to mollycoddle a dog; they are cunning animals who soon realise who is a soft touch. So, firmness is not cruelty, it is the only way to show your dog that you mean business and expect him to behave in a socially acceptable way if he is to live in your world.

The last trap that dog owners fall into is inconsistency and this, in dog training, is easy but disastrous. He may make you laugh with his sneaky antics to get onto the sofa and you may think 'I'll let him this once and pretend I haven't noticed'. Then you take him to a friend's house and there he is – all dirty paws and smug – on her cream sofa. If you chastise him now, you really are being cruel. He doesn't know an expensive sofa from a twenty-year-old wreck of a couch. It's all the same to him.

By now, the message should be loud and clear. Are you really prepared to spend time and patience, and be firm and consistent? If you are, you are a responsible dog owner and deserve the loyal, obedient and socially acceptable friend that your trained dog will be.

This book is written for you.

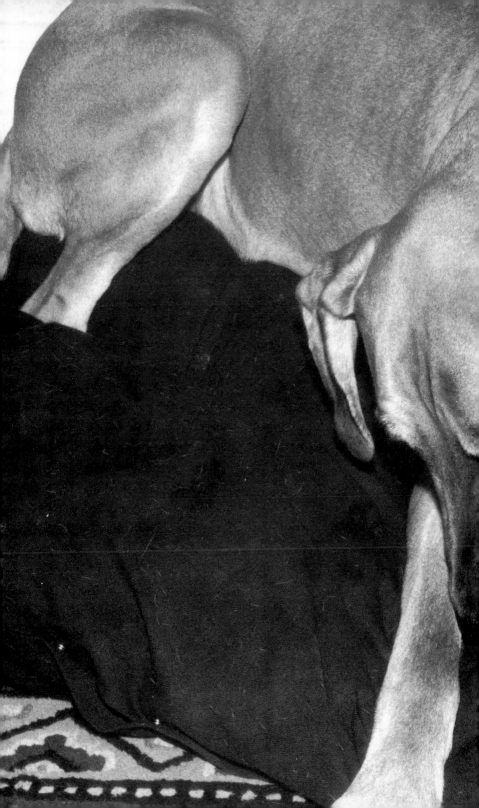

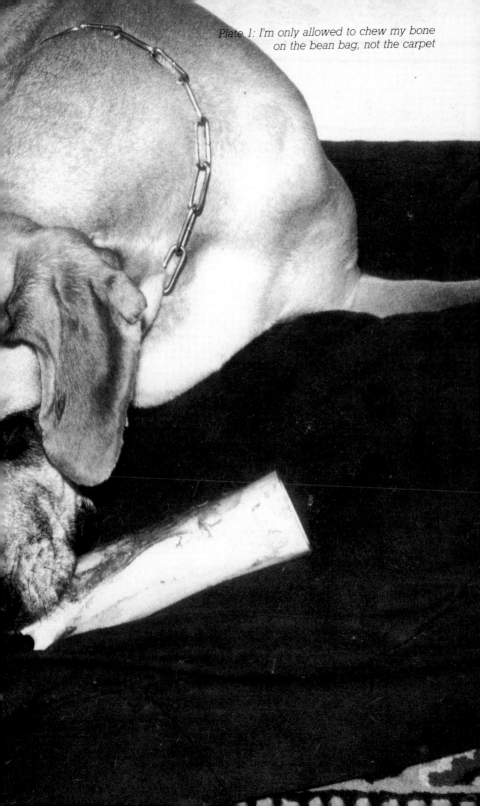

Plate 1: I'm only allowed to chew my bone
on the bean bag, not the carpet

1 Basic Commands and Signals

This is the only chapter for which you do not need a dog, so enjoy it. All you need is a basic memory and perhaps a family conference, which can be quite fun. The importance of consistency will become obvious as you decide which commands you will use and see the importance of sticking to them – you and every member of the family.

First, put yourself in the dog's mind. You do not and will never understand the meaning of words. You can, however, be taught to respond to a sound coupled with a tone of voice. Your owner teaches you to lie down by saying 'down' in a firm voice and pushing you to the floor. After a few lessons, you realise that 'down' spoken in a firm voice means that you lie down; your owner says 'clever dog!' Then, there you are, paddling a comfy circle on the sofa and your owner yells 'down'. Oh, yes, you know what down means. So you do exactly as you are told and lie down immediately – on the sofa. You don't understand English, so 'down' means only one thing to you.

Imagine yourself in a worse position. Now you are a family dog, eager to please everyone. One family member teaches you to sit by saying 'sit' and raising one finger. You get that right and are praised. Then he teaches you to lie down by saying 'down' and pointing at the floor. You learn that, too. Then another member of the family says 'sit' and points to the floor. Now, here's a puzzle, the finger says 'lie down' but the voice says 'sit'. Whatever are you to do?

Both authors have, at different times, had impeccably trained dogs that friends tried to handle and then maintained 'won't do anything'. You know the type of person, usually dashing everywhere, overpowering and unwilling to listen. So they bound up to a trial standard dog and, using the wrong tone of voice, give a command that the dog simply does not understand; a favourite is 'sit down' with arms waving everywhere. If they would only stop and listen, it can be explained to them that they have just asked the dog to do something impossible – sit and lie down at the same time. Amy, the fawn Great Dane in this book has an answer; she hides as much of herself as possible behind her owner's legs and barks at the offender in annoyance. Such people perpetuate the myth that the dog won't obey anyone but its owner. This may be true in very rare cases, but in the vast majority it is not. A well-trained dog will respond to anyone who knows the correct commands, signals and tone of voice with which he was trained.

Now that the importance of consistency in commands is clear, decide which you are going to use and stick to them – you and every member of the family. As a dog only reacts to the association of a sound with an action, you can use any words you choose as long as you do not vary them. There are, however, definite disadvantages in choosing silly words as no one wants to be heard calling 'drawers' in the park if that is the word chosen to mean 'sit'.

We use the basic commands and hand signals listed in the table. If you want to change these, there is a space at the side to write in your own words.

These basic commands and hand signals are all you will need to teach in order to achieve good behaviour. But why the hand signals for sit, down and stay? There are different reasons depending upon whether you are inside or outside. Indoors, the reason is social. Sharp verbal commands are a bit off-putting when you have visitors or are in someone else's house. How many times have you had to talk over someone shouting 'down', 'sit' etc to a badly behaved dog? With a trained dog there is no need for it. You surreptitiously raise a finger and the dog sits. Or you point to the floor and he lies down – no noise, no fuss.

In the open, hand signals can save your animal's life. A recent, sad story concerns a young couple, devoted to their dog. The man was out walking him at the edge of the park, off the lead, when his wife, out shopping, appeared across the road. The dog saw her and made off towards her. The wind

Basic Commands and Signals

was in the wrong direction for him to hear the man calling and he couldn't hear the wife for the traffic. They saw him run over and killed. Had the dog been trained with hand signals for 'sit' or 'down', he might have survived, as the wife could have tried a hand signal as she saw him run towards her.

And don't forget the last, but most important words, though they don't require the dog to do anything apart from wag his tail and lick your hand. They are 'good girl' or 'good boy', said in the jolliest voice you can muster, together with a ruffling of the ears.

Command and tone of voice	Position you want the dog to adopt	Hand signal	Your command if different
'SIT' Firm and sharp. Normal voice but clearly pronounced			
'DOWN' Very firm and slightly threatening			
'OFF' Firm and sharp like 'sit'	When dog is expected to get off something, eg furniture	None	
'LEAVE' Firm and sharp	When dog is expected to drop some-thing it has in its mouth/is about to reach for, or doing some-thing you wish it to stop	None	

14

SUMMING-UP

The commands must be given consistently and in the right tone of voice. Firmness first, followed by immediate praise when the dog gets it right. He may not know the meaning of 'what a good dog' but if you say the word as if you really *are* pleased, he'll know immediately that you are happy with him.
Now you can start to practise on the dog.

Command and tone of voice	Position you want the dog to adopt	Hand signal	Your command if different
'COME' Friendly and inviting	When you want the dog to come back to you	None	
'HEEL' Firm and sharp		None	
'STAY' Firm but **gentle**	When you want the dog to stay in a standing position		
'UP' Firm and sharp	When you want the dog to jump, eg into the back of the car	None	
'ON YOUR BED' Firm	Obvious	None	
'QUIET'	Obvious	None	

2 Car Training

Importance and general tips

Car training is important for two reasons. First, for your dog's sake so that he can spend as much time as possible with you rather than be left at home when you're out for the day, or left in kennels if you are staying in a hotel that does not take dogs. Second, it means you are still able to go out, visit friends and stay away from home; to carry on your normal lifestyle, which is how it should be. People who say 'I can't do this or that because of the dog' are really saying 'I haven't spent time training my dog so I find it easier not to go anywhere'. Do not be sympathetic.

To a properly trained dog, the car is simply a mobile kennel and he is very happy to travel and sleep overnight in it. You can, therefore, stay in hotels or with friends, for limitless periods, with the dog sleeping in the car at night and out exercising with you during the day.

CAR TRAINING DO'S AND DON'TS

● After the sun has gone down, a dog is perfectly safe in the car as long as a window is down a crack for ventilation. This applies to all weathers **apart** from sub-zero temperatures. When it is above zero, but very cold, supply warm blankets and, ideally, a cheap single duvet. In sub-zero temperatures many long-haired dogs are still warm and happy, but it is not worth taking the risk unless your dog has always been kennelled outside and you know he is used to sudden and violent drops in temperature.

● Do not expect a dog to stay in the car all day as well as night as he will become bored and unhappy. If he is being asked to sleep in the car, it is only fair to devote at least half of the preceding day to him. For example, give him a few hours running and playing and then put him back in the car for the same period. By ensuring that he is in and out of the car at regular intervals during the day you will make him realise that, although you leave him, you'll soon be back for another walk and a game.

● Dogs die quickly in very hot cars. In the summer, you may feel that the car is cool enough when you stop, but this is only because it has been moving with the windows open. Leave it with the window down a crack for quarter of an hour in direct sun and it becomes a greenhouse. Always park in the shade in warm weather but *look to see where the sun is*. A car in the shade of a wall at 11am is in full sun at midday, an hour later. You could return at two in the afternoon, after leaving your dog for three hours, to a tragedy.

Getting him used to the car

Car training should begin the day after you bring the dog home. If you picked him up in the car, chances are he will associate it with feeling sick or miserable. Because of this, he may not be eager to get back in again. Do not give in and feel you are being cruel by forcing him into the car again so soon, you are not. First, exercise the dog and tire him a little before going to the car. Decide where you will want him to travel in the future – in the back of an estate or on one side of the back seat in a saloon (never in the front). Place the dog's blanket on the chosen spot and put him on it. Comfort him, tickle him and try to settle him. Then close the door with you outside. Do not go out of sight; he must know at this stage that you are not deserting him. Walk around the car and use the chance to check tyres, mirrors or maybe to wash the car. Obviously if you wash the car, do not use a high pressure hose and scare him.

He will probably do one of two things. He will whine and look pathetic and then settle down, or he will go beserk, throwing himself around the car. If he settles, you're in luck. You've got a dog that will take to car training easily. Leave him for an hour in the car, always staying in sight in case he wakes up. Then take him out of the car and make a fuss of him.

If you're in the majority and your dog is doing an impression of an insane stuntman, steel yourself. You're in for a hard time; but be reassured. We've been through it with several dogs and won in the end – with patience. Take a deep breath (you must **never** frighten him by showing real anger) and open the door. Grab the ball of fury next time he sails past you, say 'no' firmly, plonk him on his blanket and close the door again. Whatever you do, no matter how tempted, do not cuddle him or sound inviting. If you do, he will think he has won and that his screaming and gyrations have brought the desired result.

If he settles the second time, leave him for about a quarter of an hour and then get him out and make a fuss of him. Put him back in and soldier on for an hour until he really gets the message that if he's good and stays quiet, you come back and cuddle him; if he doesn't you aren't nice to him. If he doesn't settle the second time he may carry on going berserk for an hour. If this happens, you simply soldier on with the procedure for an hour. No one would say that this type of dog personality is easy. You will be frazzled and exhausted and probably close to losing your temper. The neighbours may be finding the procedure highly amusing and the street may be assembled outside the car with sandwiches and flasks to watch the entertainment. If you're the sensitive type, your only option is to drive to somewhere where no one knows you.

Whichever dog type you have, you must practise this training with him as often as possible. The good one needs to know it's for keeps and the middling to bad one has still to learn that you are determined and will not let him control you. A general rule is to practise the hour exercise at least three times a week for a month. By the end of this time, your dog will feel comfortable in the car and, very important, you will have proved to him that you aren't deserting him for ever when the door closes, so he gains confidence.

When you reach the stage where it seems that the dog has settled for a few lessons running, you can start to get him used to the car moving. Get in, start the engine and move the car backwards and forwards a few times (only a few yards). As you do it, comfort him with soft voice praise. If the neighbours are around they really love this bit. If he bounces into the front seat of the car, or starts putting his paws on the back of your seat, say 'no', stop the car, put him back on his blanket and say 'sit' firmly. This exercise is easiest with two people for obvious reasons, but do not let whoever is dog-handling allow the dog to get off the blanket and onto a lap. It can be very tempting as he will certainly behave and be very sweet and appealing in someone's arms. But all you are teaching him to do is create merry hell when the person is taken away and he is back with only a blanket for company.

Car Training

When the dog is behaving fairly well (staying on his blanket for the vast majority of the time) you will be relieved to know that you can begin proper drives with him and get away from the amused looks and snide remarks. Start with a drive of around 2 miles (3.2km), still keeping to the previous procedures if he steps out of line. Before setting off, make sure that he has been well exercised and hasn't eaten in the previous 2 to 2½ hours. He may dribble, or be a little sick, but apart from the mess, this is of no concern. He will soon get over it when he gets used to travelling. After a few of these practice drives you can start to take him out with you for the evening. Take a bottle of water and a heavy bowl. Leave in plenty of time; you owe it to him to allow time to talk to him and settle him properly before leaving him for a while in strange surroundings.

When you arrive, put water in the bowl on the floor and show him where it is. With a small puppy, it is sensible to put your finger in the bowl and drip some water on his nose gently so he licks it off and realises what you are showing him. Put him on his blanket and talk to him for a minute in a reassuring voice. Every hour, go back to check on him and ensure all is well. If he's asleep, leave him well alone. If you wake him by approaching the car and he starts to whine and cry at you, open the door and talk to him and fondle him for a minute. Do not take him out. Then place him firmly back on his blanket and leave him again. One note of caution. Before you drive off at the end of the evening, do not forget to empty the water bowl!

If you follow these rules and have managed to be firm, patient and persistent against all odds, you will find that you have a dog that will both behave in the car and sleep happily in it all night. Your devotion has paid dividends – how many of your mocking neighbours have dogs that behave that well in the car?

Curing the car 'barker'

A real menace in the car is the barker and whiner; he is not only a nuisance to the owner and the driver, he is also a potential road hazard. For some dogs – and it has nothing to do with breed, but temperament and personality – a simple, firm 'quiet' repeated a few times when he starts to bark is sufficient. The usual reason for barking and whining is over-excitement caused by a familiar routine. If the dog knows that every time he gets into the car at 9am he is going to the park, he will become excited and bark. Or if one partner always takes the dog to the station at a certain time to meet the other partner, the same thing happens. Routines must be varied in order that the dog does not associate the car and a certain time with something he likes so much that he barks or whines with excitement.

Some dogs bark incessantly at other dogs seen through the windows; this can and must be stopped, although you will have to accept a damp car for a few days. Fill a well-washed washing-up liquid bottle (or a pump spray bottle) with water and drive to a spot where you know there will be many dogs passing, for example outside a park. Stop and turn off the engine. When the dog starts to bark, say 'quiet' in hard, firm, clearly pronounced tones. The very moment the words have been said, squirt him full in the face with water. As the next dog approaches, say the same word but do not squirt him; just show him the bottle and make sure he has seen it. If he carries on barking, squirt him again. If he doesn't, praise him as hard as you can in the most enthusiastic voice you can muster. This water treatment has to be repeated until he will allow other dogs to walk past him without barking. Even when the lesson is learned, keep the bottle in the car to shake at him as a warning. He'll soon associate it with the command 'quiet'.

If you really can't face a few squirts of water in the car, use a similar but not quite so effective method with a check chain (page 60) and long lead replacing the plastic bottle and water. Where before you would have squirted him, now give a sharp tug on the check chain at the same time as the command.

Don't think that either method is cruel or will harm your dog. Remember, it is for his own good, too, and such lessons are but a very short part of his life. Once learned, he will retain them forever.

REMIND YOURSELF THAT CAR BARKERS ARE:

● likely to hurt themselves by throwing themselves around in a frenzy;
● often, by distracting the driver, the cause of road accidents that harm adults, children and other dogs;
● likely to be left alone, shut in a house, because the owner cannot stand the noise in the car;
● a nuisance when left outside a friend's house where the owner has been invited to dinner.

Dog gates

By now, you will probably be wondering why dog gates haven't been mentioned. Dog gates are commonly used and, to most of the dog-owning public, are the first pre-requisite. But a trained dog is preferable to a caged one. People put cages in their cars usually because the dog will not stay where it is put unless caged. The training such dogs receive is nil. In time, many of them learn to accept that they have to stay in the cage, but they learn because they try to escape and simply cannot because the bars·are too strong. They have, therefore, learnt submission rather than co-operation. Training is a co-operation between dog and owner, submission is undignified for the dog and usually unnecessary.

It often results in a dislike of the car and in non-understanding owners saying that the dog creates in the car 'and I don't know why, he's got plenty of space'. His dislike is easy to understand. He has been pushed into an alien environment, behind bars, and left to sort the problems out for himself. For those who will not accept this basic principle, there are other strong reasons against dog gates. Firstly if the car is involved in a tail-end crash the dog can be trapped. Secondly, behind a dog gate he cannot protect your car and thieves know that. There have been occasions when radios have been taken out of cars that have had noisy, fierce dogs safely caged in the rear.

For those who are still unconvinced, or need a specialist dog gate or cage for genuine reasons, there are three main types available:

Fixed: these can be ordered at the same time as the new car or fitted by the garage to an existing car.

Cages: these are free-standing, come in several sizes and go in the back of estate cars. They are available from specialist manufacturers that a good breeder could recommend to you. They have two advantages. First, the whole tailgate can be left up for ventilation if you are leaving the dog in the car. Second, if you have two dogs that are likely to fight in the car, one can go in the cage.

Adjustable: these are usually useless with large dogs, who push them over with ease.

Jumping into the car

Some dogs do not automatically jump into cars and need to be trained to do it. This is particularly important with large breeds as it takes a weightlifter to manhandle a 12-month-old Rottweiler or Dane. Up to the age of 6 months it is better to lift a puppy in as its bones are still soft, and jarring movement can be damaging. This is particularly true with the long-legged breeds like Irish Wolfhounds and Great Danes. At 6 months, the dog should jump in and out of the car on the command 'up'. The same command is used for both in and out because, to the dog, jumping is jumping, in whatever direction! Be careful, however, not to allow a dog this age to jump from too great a height or jump too frequently. A puppy's leg bones are still soft and it's easy to damage his legs.

If you have difficulty getting the dog to jump in automatically, there are several methods by which you can teach him. Arm yourself with one of his favourite toys, or a piece of food if he is more stomach- than game-oriented. Put the dog on his lead. Open the door or tailgate and take the dog back 5 to 7yd (4.5 to 6m). Show him the toy or food and walk briskly with him towards the open door. When you get there, give the command 'up' and throw the toy or food into the car (if he only responds to sticky buns you're in for a mess). In the majority of cases, the dog will be concentrating so hard on reaching the toy or food that he will not even realise that he has jumped into the car.

This will work with nearly all dogs, but it didn't wash with Amy. She was much less interested in food and toys than she was in sticking as close as possible to her owner's legs. With her we had to use another method as, at 9st (57kg) in weight, it wasn't exactly possible to go on lifting her in. Get a friend who doesn't know the dog well to help you. Put the dog on a long lead and give it to the friend. Get into the car yourself, leaving the door open and call the dog. As it reaches the door, give the command 'up'. It should jump in to reach you.

With both methods, keep on practising until the dog jumps in on the command of 'up' with no inducement. Every time it does jump into the car, give much noisy praise. Again, be careful because of his legs; one or two jumps a session are enough.

When he jumps in and out on command, you should take training a stage further by teaching social behaviour when approaching the car. He should not leap in the moment the door is opened, but should wait in a controlled manner until you have taken off your coat, stowed it and are ready for him to get in by giving the command. When you reach the car, put him into either the 'sit' or 'down' position. Open the door and leave it wide while you take off your coat and generally waste time for a few minutes. Then give the command 'up' for him to get in. After basic heel work is learnt and the 'sit' and 'down' are mastered this will be easy. One note of caution. While the dog is waiting in a controlled manner, you should keep an eye out for other dogs approaching nearby. Many big dogs are very protective of their car as it becomes their 'kennel' and a dog prone to fighting is likely to do so when he thinks another dog is approaching his home.

As well as jumping in and out on command a dog **must** be taught to stay in the car when the door or tailgate is opened until you give the command of 'up', telling him he may now jump out. Many dogs are killed and cause serious road accidents by leaping out the moment the door is opened. This is worth remembering when you are tempted to be amused at how eager he is to jump out and get into the park. You would not be amused trying to change a wheel on the motorway when every time you reached into the car for something you had to fight the dog off.

Partly open the door and give the stern command of 'sit'. If he tries to get out, push the door until it is nearly closed (being careful not to trap him). Repeat the command. Partly open the door again, repeating the command as you do so. Continue to open the door slowly and repeat the command as necessary. Leave the door open with him sitting inside for about 15 to 20 seconds and then tell him to jump out, giving lots of praise. If he jumps out before the command is given, put him back in the car and start again.

SUMMING-UP

It is a joy to see a large dog that has good car manners. He approaches the car without jumping up – he walks slowly towards it and sits patiently while the door is opened and his owner gets himself organised. Then on the command 'up' he jumps into the car and settles down where he is supposed to be. During the journey he stays in one place and does not leap around. When the car arrives at the destination, he stays still, even when all the doors are opened, until he hears the command 'up'.

Like all aspects of dog training, this takes patience. But the reward is a dog that is not only a pleasure to take out, but one that is safe for human beings on the road.

---

3 Training in the Home

Sharing your home with a big dog that has no social graces is a living nightmare. Even if the owners are prepared to put up with it, they soon find that friends and visitors are not. Ultimately, the dog suffers. He is shut away when visitors come and feels he is being banished, but hasn't a clue why. When his owners go out, he is left behind as he cannot be trusted to behave in someone else's home. So, teaching good manners around the home is as important as all other aspects of training, for your sake and the dog's – he is a sociable animal that does not like long periods alone.

You may have trained many medium-sized dogs in the home, but you'd be amazed and chastened to see the havoc the 4-month-old Amy Dane could create in minutes. There are marked differences in training a large dog rather than a small-to-medium one to be socially acceptable; young spaniels can't reach easily to 'goose' guests, can't steal from the kitchen without a ladder, nor are they strong enough to remove every drawer from a cabinet and use them as battering rams to wreck the rest of the furniture. This chapter owes its existence to Amy, who tried everything possible to turn her home into a bomb site and drive her owner to distraction.

The first point to bear in mind is that it is *your* home that you are prepared to share with the dog. You have a right to expect from him exactly the behaviour that you would expect from guests. You would not tolerate guests standing on your sofa or beds, burying bones under your cushions, howling and screaming, scratching and chewing the carpets, stealing or thrusting unwelcome attentions on you. You should not tolerate such behaviour in a dog, either.

(pp28–9) Plate 2: Playing can be a fun part of training

Furniture and beds

Many big breeds do not like lying on a carpet as it is simply not comfortable. Breeds with big angular joints and heavy bodies such as Rottweilers and Danes develop pressure sores when made to lie on carpets or bare floors for long periods of time. Unless, therefore, you provide something comfortable, you will have a very difficult job training the dog to stay off the furniture. Many people provide one dog bed, placed somewhere like the kitchen. They then spend most of their time in the lounge in front of the TV. The dog, if it loves its owner, wants to be with him as much as possible. So for him, it's a choice between his comfy bed or being with his favourite person. Usually he will choose the person and, if the room has not got a dog bed, he will try to get on the furniture. There is no rule that says a dog can only have one bed. Amy Dane has three – one in the lounge, one in the kitchen and one in the study. It is not an extravagance; it keeps her off the furniture and it helped in initial training. 'On your bed' never meant she was being sent away out of the room; when she was young and vulnerable her owner was always in sight.

The beds do not have to be expensive. Bean bags are very good for big dogs and easy to make if money is a problem. If decor is your worry, you can always cover the lounge bean bag in the same fabric as the suite or curtains so that it blends in; provide a small sofa if space is not a problem or simply drag the kitchen bean bag into the lounge when you are going in there for most of the evening.

So, assuming that there is a dog bed available close by and you have already started teaching the 'down', you can start to teach the commands 'off' and 'on your bed'. As soon as the dog puts one paw on the sofa, say 'off' sternly and remove the paw or dog. Take him by the collar (or carry him if he is a small puppy) and put him on his own bed, saying 'on your bed', then 'down'. Praise him highly with one hand on his collar to keep him down. Make sure he does lie down on the bed before leaving him and going back to your chair. If he does bounce straight off it doesn't matter as long as it isn't to go straight back onto the furniture; if it is, you must repeat the procedure immediately – 'off', then 'on your bed' then 'down'. This sounds easy, but in reality it isn't. A very bouncy, large puppy can be removed from the sofa forty to fifty times in an evening and this is one of the aspects of dog training that takes the utmost fortitude and persistence on your part. You must not give up for the sake of peace or your favourite TV programme.

After a week of total exhaustion Amy was still bouncing off her bed back onto the sofa. She then tried a different tack by employing fast bursts of speed round the room, bouncing on and off all the furniture, nipping everyone hard as she flew past, on the principle that speed would mean she couldn't be caught. With a puppy like this it is crucial that you do not inadvertently allow this to become a game, with the puppy running and you chasing. Stand your ground calmly, wait until he passes within reach, grab him by the collar with both hands and shake him hard. Then calmly lead him to his bed with the usual commands. With a puppy, persistence is the only answer.

An older dog can be nasty when removed from the sofa if he feels that he is stronger or more dominant than the owner. With such a dog, allow him into the lounge for only short periods while you are in there; never allow him in alone. Put him on a check chain with long lead and settle down holding the lead. When he goes to get on the furniture, allow him to, but the moment all four legs are up give a very hard tug on the check chain with the command 'off' and firmly, on his lead, take him to his own bed using the commands as before. Don't forget the praise when he is on his own bed even if you are cross with him for growling at you. Alternatively, you can use the basic training technique of throwing the lead at him as explained on page 66. Wait until he has all four paws up then call 'off'. If he does not respond immediately, throw the lead at him *hard*.

Training in the Home

It is important that the dog is not made to believe that his bed is a punishment, so that as well as involving his bed in furniture training, you show him that it is really a good place to be and where nice things happen. Occasionally, arm yourself with two nice titbits and show them to him. Then say 'on your bed' and walk towards it. When he is on the bed, either sitting or lying, give him the titbit and praise him. Give him the second one while he is still on there. Eventually you will show him a titbit and he will automatically go to his bed and lie down expectantly.

If you have done as suggested and have a bean bag or bed in your lounge, you can reach the stage where he will chew a bone on his bed without dropping it on the carpet. When he drops it over the side, simply pick it up, put it on the bed with him and say 'on your bed'. If Amy accidently drops a bone over the side of her bed, she now leans down and carefully picks it up herself as her owner calls 'good girl' from the comfort of the sofa.

Once the dog has mastered 'on your bed' you can really start to enjoy his company in the evenings. Sometimes he will choose to sleep across your feet, sometimes he will lie in front of the fire or he will settle on his bed. But he won't be on your furniture or driving your guests to distraction – he knows his place.

Recall and obedience

Recall training should be started the moment the puppy arrives. Get his meal ready and make sure he sees you have it in your hand. Then get another person to take the puppy to the other side of the room. Show him the bowl and tap it on the floor to get his attention. Call his name, immediately followed by 'come', just as the other person releases him. Repeat 'come' a few times as he comes towards you. Grab him just before he reaches the bowl and make a fuss of him before he is allowed his dinner.

Practise with his toys. Show him something he likes to play with and say 'come'. Use biscuits or titbits; they don't do any harm at this stage. What you are teaching him is that 'come' means he'll get something nice if he comes back to you.

Obedience training in the home, however, does not have to be confined to the recall. As 6-month-old Amy learnt new exercises outside, they were also practised inside. As a result, she is now able to play with toys indoors, even at her size, and not create havoc. For example, she would be given the 'sit' command and signal. Most of the time she sat and waited (with some wriggling and I can't help it but I must get up). A toy was then thrown to a part of the room well away from the china cabinet. Not only did this give her practice and fun, it meant that she was controlled and not throwing her considerable bulk all around the room while she was waiting for a game. She is 4 years old now and still plays in the house, but in a slightly more advanced way because it's done silently, on hand signals. It's good practice and intellectual interest for the dog and minimal effort on the part of the owner!

So, formal training does not all have to happen out of doors; practise in the home as well.

'Leave'

All dogs must be taught that on the command 'leave' they must drop whatever they are holding or stop the action they are doing (or about to do). While you may be able to prise open the jaws of an adult spaniel to extract a strange or dangerous object, try it with a fully grown Rottweiler or Doberman! And if your year-old Dane is cleaning out the ears of a guest that doesn't like dogs, just try stopping it with brute strength alone.

Start to teach 'leave' by making a game of it. Throw a ball or soft toy and when the dog has it firmly in his jaws, say 'leave' and try to take it out of his mouth. If he pulls and clamps his jaws, place your hands as shown (Plate 3) pushing the thumb and fingers of one hand in the back of his jaws, saying 'leave', sternly. He will either let go, or if he's a tough one, hold harder. If he holds harder, squeeze until you push his jowls onto his teeth to make him let go. He may yip; does it hurt? Yes, it does, a bit. But better that now than his swallowing something dangerous, and dying because you hadn't taught him to leave on command. With some dogs, even this fails. If so, you have no choice but to hit him hard across the nose. But do be careful. As his 'best friend' you will be allowed to do this and be 'forgiven' very quickly. Do *not* allow friends or acquaintances to do it as it will only make him afraid of people, and more likely to snap.

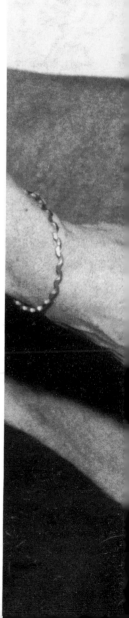

Plate 3: 'Leave'

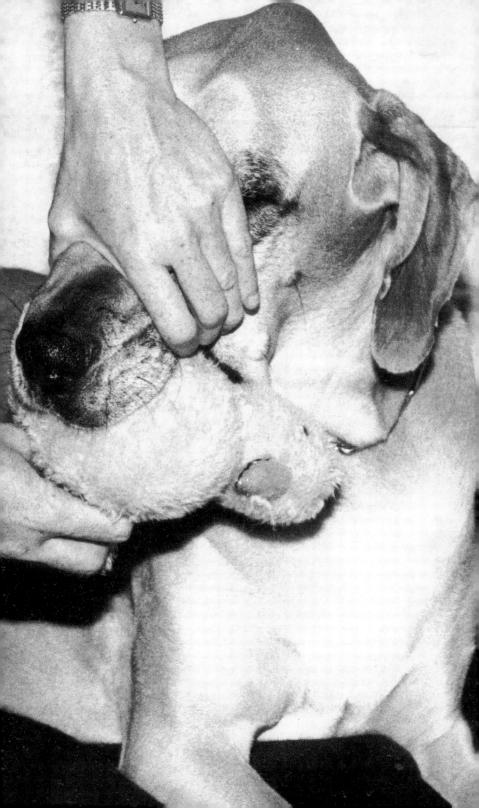

Training in the Home

As soon as you have extracted the object, make an enormous fuss of him and throw it again. This time, let him play with it for a while before you say 'leave'. Keep this up and you'll soon find he responds to the 'game'.

One word of warning with a puppy. Do not, immediately after a 'leave', put the object away out of sight. If you do, he'll associate 'leave' with losing something he likes. So if you've been playing with a squeaky toy that is driving you to total distraction, make sure you let him play with it for some minutes after the last 'leave' so that he doesn't get the wrong idea and always hangs on for grim death.

Unless you are training a dog for trials, when you must devote a massive amount of time and effort to training, do not be upset if you do not achieve total perfection in the 'leave'. Amy and her best friend Daley (a Weimeraner) were similar ages and received identical training. When they were out together, Daley could be 100yd (90m) away carrying a ball and would drop it immediately on the command of 'leave'. Amy would not, until she could see the whites of her owner's eyes and knew it was really serious. The difference was purely in terms of personality – Daley was not a competitive 'pack leader'. He was a very decent chap, but Amy was the archetypal 'pack leader' and an acquisitive horror. Her owner could have the ball, but there was no way she would drop it if Daley was closer. If you have a 'pleasant' dog, you can aim for immediate 'leave' under any circumstances. If you have a 'pack leader' you can aim for a reluctant, but nevertheless successful, 'leave' with other dogs in sight and an immediate 'leave' when you are alone with the dog or very close to him.

Stealing

Who wouldn't be tempted to take a tasty morsel within easy reach? A joint of beef or a pound of cheese at convenient nose-height to an Irish Wolfhound or a mere stretch to a German Shepherd can be just too much to resist. But stealing has to be prevented for the sake of the dog as much as for your own. A dog that helps itself becomes obese, anti-social and may, one day, even help itself to something dangerous and die.

The first rules are simple. Never allow him to eat anything he has stolen. From your point of view he might as well, as you won't eat it after it's been in his mouth. But from his point of view he'll take it to mean that he always gets what he steals and is on to a good thing. At 6 months old, Amy bounded into the lounge and proudly dropped a pound and a half of cheese onto the sofa, still in the cellophane but well punctured. It was such an endearing action – she was simply asking nicely if she could have it – but, tempting though it was to let her have just a little, she was scolded and it was put in the fridge to mix with her dinner.

Never allow a dog to eat anywhere apart from where he always has his main meals. If you choose to allow him to eat his bones or chews on his bed, this should be the only exception; he can cope with understanding two places are 'allowed' but is unlikely to be able to cope with more than that. Even the smallest titbit anywhere else must be denied. If you give him, for example, biscuits from your coffee table when he is young, you'll spend the rest of your life with him drooling over your feet (and the table) as you try to watch TV eating a bar of chocolate.

The danger areas are obviously the kitchen, dining area and coffee table. Keeping the surfaces clear of food while the dog or puppy is around is not a long-term answer. The day comes when you are preparing a meal for guests and can't be in the kitchen and dining room at the same time. Amy was adept at

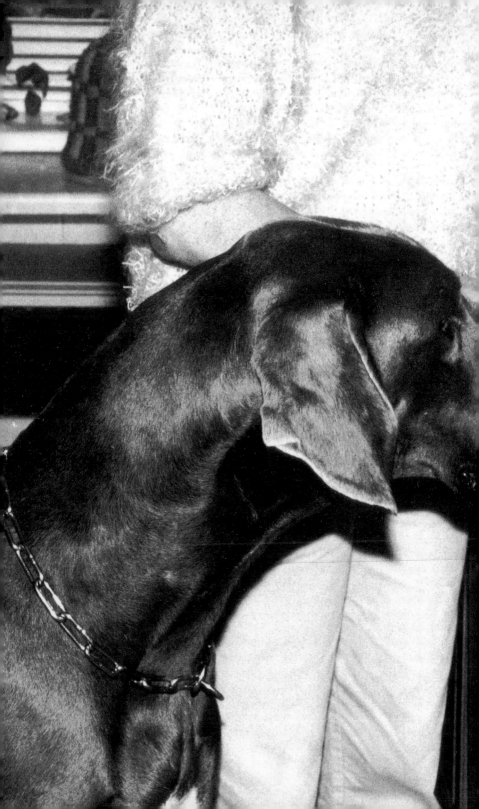

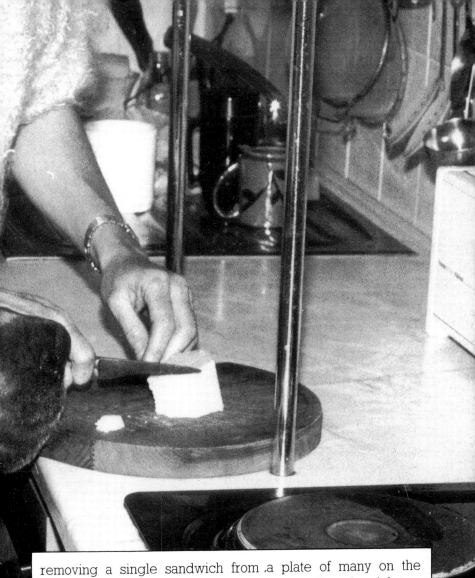

removing a single sandwich from a plate of many on the kitchen hatch in the time it took anyone to walk to the sink two yards away. And the look of innocence was quite believable until a sandwich count was done.

There are two stages to go through. First you have to teach the young puppy to leave food alone when you are present. Then you have to teach him to leave it when you are out of sight.

Plate 4: Look – no need to stretch!

THE KITCHEN

Start teaching before the puppy is big enough to reach the working surfaces. All puppies jump up, trying to see what is going on and it is this that has to be stopped. Keep a pump spray bottle (the type used in the garden) full of clean water on the hatch. As soon as paws are put up and a nose sniffs the air (even if you are preparing *his* food) say 'leave' and push him firmly back onto all four paws. It won't work; he'll bounce up again. Try once more. When he bounces again, spray him full in the face, at the same time saying 'leave'. Keep it up until he gives up – any time from a day to five months! Eventually 'leave' and just seeing the spray bottle will work, then just 'leave' alone. In the long term, wet shoes, floor and clothes are a small price to pay for obedience.

Now he doesn't jump up while you're in the kitchen, but try leaving the room and you'll probably come back to find him scrabbling the sides of the units to see if he just might reach. Now is the time, before he can reach, for him to learn that you can 'see' through walls, which he will find very disconcerting. Leave him in the kitchen with something interesting on the worktop and go just outside, leaving the door open. The moment you hear his claws click on the side of the cupboard, shout 'leave'. Most dogs are so startled that they stop, but if yours doesn't, you'll have to dash back into the room and shake him. Keep up the technique for 'seeing through walls' and you'll convince him he's never really out of your sight. Eventually, you'll come back into the room to find him sitting patiently, looking at the surface or at the door, waiting for you to appear.

As he grows and his nose reaches the surface without jumping up, temptation usually takes over again, which is easy to understand. Watch him like a hawk. By the time he is big enough to reach the surface he should already know the

Plate 5: Give me two more months . . .

40

Training in the Home

command 'leave'. With some dogs it is sufficient. With others, a return to the spray bottle is needed, in conjunction with 'leave' as the nose reaches an inch away from the edge of the surface. Do not listen to friends who advocate sprinkling pepper; it's cruel and unnecessary. Clean water is equally effective, but is kind as it relies on startling the dog, not hurting it.

He will probably also need some intensive reminders of your ability to see through walls. As now his head is on a level with the food, there is no tell-tale sound of scrabbling claws to warn you he is about to swallow a joint of beef and prompt your 'leave'. Now you must say 'leave' before you go out of the room, ensuring he has seen what he must leave. This obviously points out the importance of teaching the leave before he is big enough to reach!

As with all dog training, some dogs learn this much faster than others. A naturally very greedy dog or one with a penchant for certain foods may take longer. Patience and reiteration are the only answers with these inveterate thieves.

Amy was moderately good at 'leave' (very few problems from 8 months onwards) even with foods she particularly liked, but she was 18 months old when she stole her last piece of Cheddar. By then, she was too wise to bring it into the lounge to show what she had. From that last slip-up at 18 months old, even cheese has been safe, but if Cheddar is left on the worktop, prepare to slip on huge pools of saliva on the floor. However, the cheese is untouched and the work surface is saliva-free. As a reward for leaving the thing she loves most in the world, she occasionally has a dog biscuit. Tempting though it is, the treat is never cheese; that would wipe out years of training in one small sliver.

THE DINING ROOM

Some people solve the problem simply by refusing to allow the dog in the dining room. This is not the answer. Not all houses have separate dining rooms and not all people live in the same houses all their lives. It is far better to train the dog to stay away from the dining table and human beings while they are eating.

Teaching dining-room manners is an identical procedure to the kitchen lesson. Always make sure the dog has had his dinner before you sit down to yours. It will make you firmer when you know he's greedy, not hungry. For a while, you'll probably have terrible indigestion as you'll be trying to eat while armed with a spray bottle, but it's worth it. The whole family must co-operate and be forbidden to even acknowledge the dog's presence apart from giving the sharp command of 'leave' as he tries to jump up and scrabble legs. If you are not hard at this stage, you'll be extremely sorry later when friends come to supper, as no one likes the constant attentions of a begging dog.

At this stage, friends can be your worst enemies. If they don't like dogs, they slip a titbit in the hope the dog will go away. If they do like dogs they start the 'one bit won't hurt' routine. Remind them very firmly that they may do what they like with their own dog, but you will not have yours fed at the table. Also remind them of the size your puppy will reach – plate height. It really is worth laying down the ground rules pleasantly before dinner, explaining the reasons why they must help you and ignore any begging on the part of the puppy. Also insist that they do the same as you – refuse to acknowledge paws on legs and push the puppy off firmly. If some friends really don't like dogs at all, it's unfair to ask them to help and, in this instance, the puppy must be shut away for the duration of dinner.

THE COFFEE TABLE

Now for the best bit. Are you used to a comfy coffee-table meal in front of the TV? If so, get ready to be thoroughly miserable for a while. When you're on a low sofa you're at an ideal height to have a nose thrust into your dinner or be dribbled on.

All the same rules apply. If you put your meal down to change channels and he pounces on it, shake him hard by the collar and deposit him away from the food. Throw the food into the bin and start again. 'Leave' and the spray bottle will replace salt and pepper for a while and you may lose some weight, but it will pay off. A TV dinner also has to be protected in case you put it down to go to the kitchen for the forgotten mustard. Rather than practise this with good food, wait until the plate is empty and put it down on the coffee table. The first few times, leave someone else in the room armed with the spray bottle. Progress to an empty room and seeing through walls, saying 'leave' before you go out to the kitchen. You may lose one or two dinners, but he will learn.

As mentioned earlier, a dog must learn that there are designated places where he may eat and nowhere else in the house. It might seem sensible, therefore, for leftover scraps from the table to be taken to his bowl in the kitchen after the meal and given to him. Amy gave a dramatic demonstration of the folly of this, however, the night her patience ran out and she pushed a guest off his chair because he was taking too long and she wanted her share taken to the kitchen. Feed scraps by all means, but keep them in the fridge until the puppy's next mealtime.

General jumping up

A puppy or dog will often jump up, putting his paws on you, either as an expression of joy or to try and reach whatever you are holding. If it's because you've just come in and you know he's really pleased to see you, it's difficult to harden your heart and stop him doing it, but you must. Remember that if he's a puppy and can only reach your knee-caps now, he won't stay that way forever. A Wolfhound, Dane or English Sheepdog puppy will grow into a dog that can put his paws on your shoulders – and he will. He'll ruin your clothing and make you late for appointments by jumping up and dirtying your clothes just as you're leaving the house all neatly dressed. He'll ruin your social life by jumping up on guests. It must be stopped. In the home, the spray-bottle technique used in curing stealing should be sufficient to stop him. But you are unlikely to have spray bottles everywhere, for example by the front door. And you won't be carrying one when you go out.

All small puppies jump up as part of play and this is perfectly normal. While the puppy is very young, discourage him only gently, by pushing his paws off and scolding him in a soft tone. By the time he is 6 to 7 months old you can, and must, start to be firmer with him.

This is going to sound cruel, but you have to accept that it really isn't. As the dog jumps up, slap it on the top of the head with the flat of your hand, saying 'no' firmly at the same time. It will not hurt him, but he won't like it, any more than you would. Bear in mind that if you hit him on the top of the head with a clenched fist, it will probably hurt you more than it hurts him. So the flat of the hand is a minor hardship and really only a scare tactic. Please don't be fooled. If he goes rushing off whimpering and crying, it's fear, not hurt. Usually, one or two slaps are sufficient to curb the habit and you'll find that, if he ever looks as if he's going to jump again, a hand lifted will deter him, without the slap. Only very occasionally will a young dog need the treatment as much as four or five times before he is cured.

Some puppies will learn quickly with their owner, but still misbehave with strangers. In this instance, you have to explain to friends that they will be doing you, and the dog, an enormous service if they slap the dog on the head immediately he tries to put his paws up.

An adult dog can be a different matter. First try the spray bottle/slapping methods but if they don't work, go to the next stage. As he leaps at you, grab both his front legs and bring your knee up firmly, but not cruelly, into his chest, quickly throwing him off as hard as you can. Very few dogs will come back a second time after this, but if yours does, do it again until he stops.

Again, the help of friends can be enlisted but you have to be very careful. With the first methods, the dog is not restrained in any way and can get away at his own pace. The moment his legs are grabbed, he is restrained and can bite the hand that is holding him in his panic to get away. So only enlist the help of strangers if you are sure your dog has a very even temperament.

If all else fails, put him on a check chain and enlist the help of someone you know the dog likes and will jump up at. Hold the lead in your right hand, and as the dog approaches the person and begins to jump up, grab the lead close to the chain with your left hand and pull sharply downwards and back-wards at the same time, giving the command 'no'. Keep it up until he stops lunging forwards.

Plate 6: Jumping up must be discouraged.

Howling at night

You may have heard of an instance where a new puppy (or adult dog) has settled immediately at night. It may happen, but it's extremely rare. The big dog is no more a culprit than his smaller brothers and sisters; we've had equally bad problems with Danes, Cavaliers, Cockers, Weimeraners, German Shepherds and mongrels. In fact, the puppy that could raise the loudest hell and and wake the neighbourhood three streets away was none of these – it was a very bossy Schitzu.

Allowing a dog to sleep in your bedroom has to be a matter of personal choice, but it really isn't the right thing to do. If he gets used to it, it makes it very difficult if you go away and try to leave him with someone else who refuses to share *his* bedroom. Also, shut in the bedroom with you, he isn't doing his job and listening in the hall for intruders. And while a small dog may curl up almost unnoticeably in a corner, you need a very big bedroom indeed to take a Rottweiler or get away from a smelly Dane that has been jumping in puddles all afternoon. The dog should settle for the night on his bed, no matter where you put it. He must learn that his bed in sight and the light out means 'go to sleep and be quiet'.

There's no magic in teaching manners at night, but you do need strong nerves and very understanding neighbours. First, you need to realise that when he screams and howls he's calling you to come to him, on his command. This is role reversal and definitely not on.

Inform the neighbours that you are about to train a puppy at night and apologise in advance for the probable noise. Most people are understanding for a few nights and don't call the police. Decide where your dog is to sleep – the kitchen if it is big enough, the hallway if it is not too draughty. Place his bed where you want him to stay and give him a bowl of water. If he's not yet housetrained, supply a few sheets of newspaper. Pat him, leave him and go to bed. He will now start to howl the place down, or he may be crafty and just whine pathetically. Ignore him completely. Try and treat it as a lesson in canine psychology and listen to the different tones he'll try for effect. Some dogs have a quite wonderful repertoire ranging from the pathetic to staccato barking, to down-and-out Hound of the Baskervilles howling. Ignore it totally for an hour and a half, by which time your nerves will be frayed and you'll be worrying about the neighbours. Now you can go to him, but remember that *he is calling you* and he has no right to do that – so you're good and angry.

His first reaction as you go through the door will be joy that his ploy has worked. You dare not, therefore, for even one second, let him think you are coming in friendship. Throw the door open in real anger and, as you do, shout 'QUIET' at the top of your voice, scoop him up (or grab him by the collar) and shake hell out of him before depositing him on his bed, screaming 'QUIET' at him again and going out, slamming the door. Be careful with the shaking. You must ensure that you do not snap his head back and forwards and hurt him; if you are picking him up bodily to shake him, be very careful of this. If he's a big puppy it's easier as you can grab him by the collar, then facing him, put both hands under his collar and shake very hard safely. The action is to frighten, not hurt.

If you keep this up and it doesn't work, it's your fault, as you're not using the right amount of anger. Most dogs are prepared to put up with a cross owner if it means the owner comes to them, so admonishments like 'naughty dog' in a raised voice are not effective. Only striking terror into the real offender will work, hard though it sounds.

It's easy to think that the puppy may end up hating you and this stops some people from being tough enough. But firm behaviour never has this result. Dogs don't really hold grudges and are still really delighted to see you in the morning after the first night's training. Just make sure you give lots of cuddles and games to prove everything is now fine.

Training in the Home

POINTS TO REMEMBER

- Work yourself up into anger that shows in your body movements and your voice.

- Don't worry that he'll 'go off you'. He won't.

- Never give him anything when you go in to 'quieten him'. Give him a biscuit once and he'll get worse, crying for titbits as well as you.

- When you shake him, do it hard, but be very careful that you don't snap his neck backwards and hurt him; you want to frighten, not hurt.

- Make an enormous fuss of him in the morning, telling him what a 'good boy' he was.

- Remember, it's your house and neither you nor the neighbours are prepared to lose sleep or be ruled by a spoiled puppy.

Indoor kennels

A large, exuberant puppy can damage or kill itself if left unconfined in the house, even for a short period. It is rare, but so devastating that indoor kennels warrant inclusion in this chapter. The only way to find out whether your large puppy will do damage to itself is to leave it for short periods while you are nearby – after first removing all the plugs from their sockets in the room he is to stay in. Make sure his bed is with him and some fresh water.

Go to another room and proceed as outlined in the section covering crying at night. The sounds coming from the room will quickly let you know whether he is just running around crying and scratching the door, or risking his life by throwing himself against the window. Amy, left alone as a puppy, would run round the walls, not differentiating between the wall and the window. After avoiding disaster only by luck, it was obvious that she had to be confined when left alone until she was older, quieter and more under control.

Up to 5 months old a large breed puppy can be left in a child's playpen as long as:

● it has a base to stop escape underneath;
● strong wire is attached all round to stop the puppy's neck getting stuck between the bars – but be careful there are no sharp ends on the inside;
● the puppy isn't left too long. At this age, up to two hours is the maximum.

A puppy that needs this kind of confinement will not be held by a playpen after 5 months. Before going to the time and trouble of indoor kennelling, try him once more unconfined in a room just in case he will now settle. If not, and outdoor kennelling is not feasible, further indoor kennelling is the only solution. There are three ways, all of which are disruptive and cause varying degrees of damage to your home!

51

Plan 1 – indoor kennel (Great Dane puppy size)

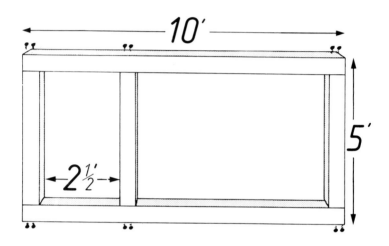

10′

5′

2½′

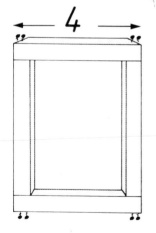

4

Two wooden frames
(1½″×1½″ or 2″×2″ wood)
screwed firmly together
with two screws
at each corner.

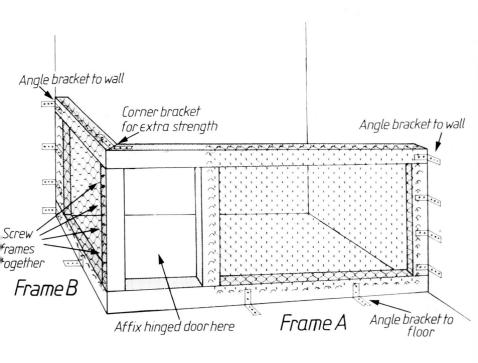

Angle bracket to wall

Corner bracket
for extra strength

Angle bracket to wall

Screw
frames
together

Frame B

Affix hinged door here

Frame A

Angle bracket to
floor

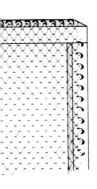

Cover each frame by stapling
heavy wire netting onto it.
BUT ensure that the wire is
secured on the edges and does
not protrude to the other side.
Leave a gap on the larger frame
'A': (2½' marked) as this will be
the entrance.

Training in the Home

The first option is to empty a room and nail hardboard halfway up the window, still allowing light in – seriously. When the puppy grows and quietens down, you remove the hardboard, fill in the holes and repaint. This relies, however, on you having somewhere else to store the contents of the room and being able to live without the use of the room for some time, which isn't always possible.

Amy could only be given half a large room, but with the furniture stacked at the other side, this is a feasible second option. She had a built-in pen, 10ft by 4ft (3 × 1.2m) tightly screwed to the wall with angle brackets. One end was her bed and the other was covered in newspaper for accidents (Plan 1). It was constructed by a woman who had only ever put up shelves before, so it shouldn't be beyond most people's DIY abilities. The main advantages of it were that it was cheap to make and very sturdy.

If money is no object, the third option is to buy a heavy-duty wire pen of the type used by breeders; yours will be able to tell you how to contact the nearest suppliers.

Please, please, do not lose sight of the objective of indoor kennelling. It is to stop a very large puppy from hurting itself when you must leave it, not to shut it away to give you peace. So do not be tempted to use the pen too much in order to get away from a boisterous puppy that is driving you insane. If you do, the puppy will never learn social behaviour, which is the ultimate aim. An indoor kennel is not there to stop the puppy wrecking furniture or chewing carpets; these things have to be taught. At regular intervals, leave the puppy out of the pen, but with the door open. And dispose of the pen immediately you judge him not to be endangering himself.

Large dogs and children

Sadly, many large dogs end up in rescue centres because a childless couple suddenly decide to have a baby and they 'don't trust the dog with the baby'. If the dog is that disposable to them, it is probable that they never deserved a dog in the first place.

There is certainly a risk of jealousy of a new baby on the part of some dogs, although most of them immediately recognise 'young' and quickly become protective of 'their' baby. Two Doberman – a male and a female – are often seen walking in West London parks with their owner, and present a heartwarming sight. 'Their' baby is in her pushchair and the Doberman run around playing some distance away. But the female never takes her eyes off the pushchair and will dash back to fend off both strange dogs and humans who get within six feet. What is important is that she warns, but is not vicious, which would be totally unacceptable. Her actions are those of a well-trained dog who has been taught that biting is not on, but warning is allowed.

The rules for integrating a new baby into a home with a large dog, without jealousy, are similar to those which introduce a toddler to a new baby. Don't devote too much time to the newcomer and make the dog feel he is neglected and that the baby is taking his rightful time and love. If anything, spend more time making a fuss of the dog than before the new arrival. Make sure the baby isn't always in your arms and don't keep snatching it way when the dog goes to look at it curiously. Be on your guard, by all means, but not allowing the dog to sniff and investigate the baby will foster dislike.

No matter how much you trust your dog's temperament, *never* leave him alone with a baby or young child. With a baby, there is the danger of suffocation if the dog decides to settle down in the cot; but, more important, a child may move quickly and startle the dog into snapping, in automatic self defence.

Training in the Home

A dog brought up in a childless home where children do not even visit, cannot be expected to understand or cope with children. It is, therefore, an important part of such a dog's early training (5 months on) that you ensure he meets and mixes with them. The best way to do this is to elicit the help of friends with a child 4 years old plus and, preferably, with dogs of their own. Such people will have already acclimatised their children to dogs and the children will know that they must not scream at them or tease them. Before the child arrives, remove all bones or toys that the dog is very fond of, to avoid squabbles. Talk to the child beforehand, telling him or her that the puppy hasn't met little girls or boys before and to be gentle and quiet. Get the child to sit on the sofa and, in the first instance, allow the puppy to come to the child, not the other way round. Under careful supervision, they'll be good friends in no time and playing together.

Amy was born at the same time as a friend's baby boy and they first met when both were 5 months old. Tom sat on his mother's lap, wearing bright red socks. Amy bounded over and everyone took a deep breath. She carefully sniffed his face, licked his ears, then gently removed one of his socks by the very tip, taking care not to nip even one tiny toe. At that time, all the humans sported Amy's puncture marks, so it proved beyond doubt that she instinctively understood Tom was only a baby and that she had to be careful with him. As the months passed, Tom would crawl at full tilt round the room with Amy bounding beside him, bending down to look into his face. At that time she was a dreadful hooligan with adults, but not once did she tread on Tom, nip him, or frighten him.

In many instances, a dog gets a bad name instead of the child getting a smacking. Even the best behaved dog can snap in fright when a child screams in his ear or grabs his nose. Dogs are trained, and children should be trained too. Seeing an adult bend over her dog from the rear a little girl in the park was heard to say 'don't do that, my mummy says dogs don't like it'. She was quite right. Children should be taught that:

Training in the Home

- Screaming or shouting close to a dog frightens it and may make it bite. Shout loud in the child's ear and ask what it felt like.
- Bending over a dog makes it feel it's going to be punished and a dog should always be approached from the front, on bended knees, with a flat hand outstretched. Do not creep up behind it.
- Dogs feel pain just like you do. Would you like someone pulling your hair or ears? Point out to a child that if they don't like something or it hurts they say so, but dogs can't and therefore they bite instead as their way of saying 'stop hurting me'.
- They must never touch a strange dog without first saying to the owner 'may I touch your dog?' in order that the owner can say 'no' if the dog is not stable with children.
- Putting their face up against the dog's is dangerous as the dog feels threatened at such closeness.
- They must never go out alone with the dog, because if he sees something interesting he'll run away and get killed.

These are only sensible basics, but it is frightening how many children have not been taught them. Amy, and now Troy, have been tested with children and passed with flying colours – little ones can ride Amy. But strangers do not know that and it is worrying that they allow their children to dash over to two massive Great Danes and grab them around the neck without asking if it is safe.

A child with a big-dog chum is a wonderful sight. Most dogs love the companionship of a child and the child learns how to treat other living things and gains a sense of responsibility in helping to train and feed the animal. It's training both of them to live together that forms the basis of such a lovely relationship.

4 Training Outside

Equipment

The equipment recommended in this section is the result of a great deal of practice, and trial and error with what is available. It is definitely false economy to buy dog-handling equipment on price alone. Cheap collars and leads do not last and, in many instances, are likely to break when there is 8st to 11st (50 to 70kg) of dog relying on them.

LEADS

1 Webbing lead, 4ft × ¾in (1.2m × 19mm) with a G-clip. This lead is very light and ideal for a puppy. It is more or less chew-proof unless the puppy steals it when you aren't looking and has time to do the damage (Fig 1).
2 Harness leather lead, 4ft × ¾in (1.2m × 19mm) with bronze G-clip and ring. This is ideal for the adult dog, and harness leather if treated with a hide food will outlive both of you. The ring on the lead allows you to clip it round you when not in use, so that you don't lose it (Fig 2).
3 Harness leather double-training lead, 6ft × ¾in (1.8m × 19mm). Unclipped, it extends, so that when teaching distance control you can get further away from the dog but still have contact via the lead (Fig 3). It is also useful if you are walking two dogs.
4 A 4ft × ¾in (1.2m × 19mm) harness leather lead with bronze G-clip and rings. This differs from lead 2 in that it has a 6in (152mm) leather loop at the clip end, which has the effect of giving a short lead and a long lead in one. Paul Dodd designed it with the help of a harness maker and calls it a 'close control' lead. It is very useful with a lively dog or one that is inclined to fight, as it is difficult for the dog to surprise you and pull it out of your hand (Fig 4). This lead is not available commercially, but any good harness maker could produce one from the drawing.

Fig 1 *An ideal puppy lead in light webbing*

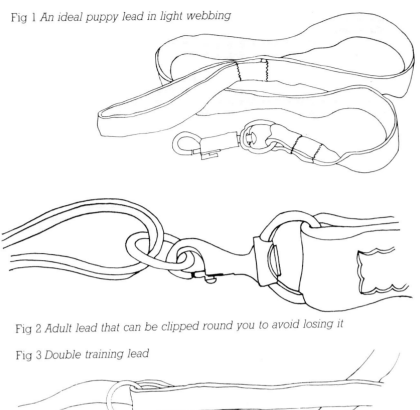

Fig 2 *Adult lead that can be clipped round you to avoid losing it*

Fig 3 *Double training lead*

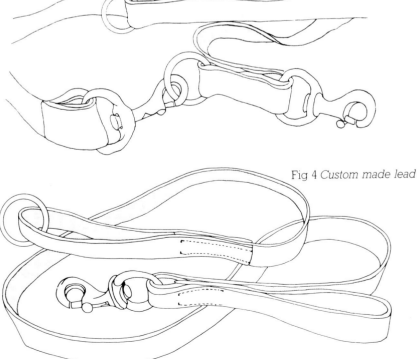

Fig 4 *Custom made lead*

COLLARS

1 A ¾in (19mm) leather collar with strong bronze clips and buckle. This is ideal for puppies (Fig 5). As the puppy grows, move up to a 1in (25mm) wide adult collar (Fig 6).
2 The wide, or long-link check chain in chromed steel, available from most pet shops.

Check the fit by pulling the chain taut – four links should be through the ring. Any longer than this and it is likely to fall off when the lead is not attached. It is very important that the check chain is fitted correctly, or it will strangle the dog and not release. See drawings for correct fitting (Fig 7, 8).

If a dog needs a check chain, this is the only one that is any good – a fine chain collar is no better for control than leather. Please remember that it is a check chain, not a choke chain. It is used only for a sharp check and then loosens, if used correctly.

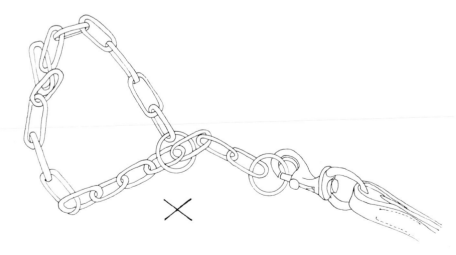

Fig 7 *Long link check chain – incorrect fitting*

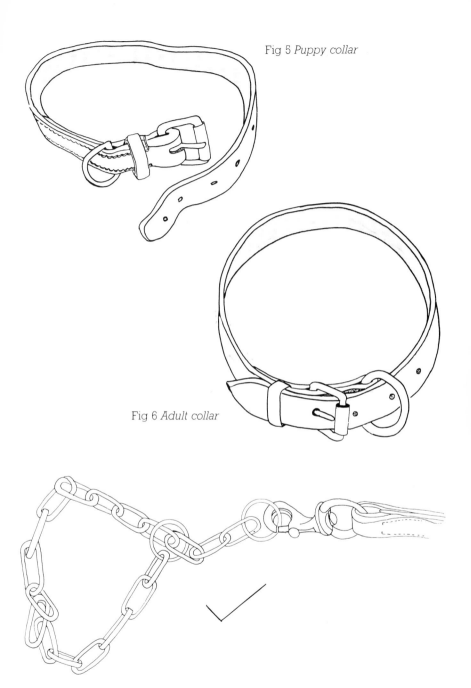

Fig 5 *Puppy collar*

Fig 6 *Adult collar*

Fig 8 *Long link check chain – correct fitting*

The first collar and lead

Basic obedience training should commence when the puppy is around 4 to 5 months old, but by this time it should already be used to wearing a light leather collar.

Buy a collar at the same time you get the puppy. Around the house, leave it quite loose while he gets used to it. The first day you take him out on a lead, tighten the collar until he is unable to back out of it. The leather collar is perfect for initial training; do not use a check chain. Choose a light lead made from nylon or webbing so that he is not weighed down unnecessarily. From the moment you clip the lead to his collar he must learn that the lead is not to be chewed. Most puppies will try, but it is a very bad habit and one you should avoid rather than have to try to break later. If he chews his lead, jerk it firmly away, saying 'leave' sternly. If he grabs it again, put your hand over his jaws, push your fingers in each side to open his mouth and pull the lead out with your other hand, saying 'leave'.

Early training on the lead (4 to 5 months)

HEELWORK

On his first few outings, the puppy will be fascinated by all the new things to look at and hear, so don't expect too much of him. Take it steadily, encouraging him, as you need to build up his confidence in this strange new world that seems enormous and confusing. It's likely that he will try to grab the lead as you walk along. Now just discourage him gently.

Hold the lead in the left hand and keep the dog at your left side. As you move off, say 'heel'. At this stage he won't have a clue what you are talking about – understanding will take some time and a few outings. If he bounds ahead, give a sharp tug (not a drag) backwards and say 'heel'. Don't keep it up for too long or keep saying 'heel' too frequently or it will just become meaningless to him. Go at a steady pace and do not let him walk with his nose to the ground or stop to sniff lamp posts (or people). He must keep his desire to sniff until he gets to the exercise area. If he keeps putting his head down, an upward tug on the lead accompanied by 'no: heel' should eventually cure him.

Some puppies will sit firmly on the ground as if to say 'I'm going nowhere with this thing round my neck'. First try encouragement and praise – 'come on, good boy' – and, if this fails, simply drag him along until he realises that it's much easier to co-operate than be dragged protesting. You must never, ever let him win, or you will be extremely sorry later. Recently, the owner of an 8-month-old Rottweiler, weighing around 80lb (36kg), asked for help. The dog had been allowed to do as he pleased on the lead, and what pleased him most was to sit down and refuse to move until the lead was removed. In the park, off his lead, he walked nicely; clip the lead on him and he promptly sat down. Cajoling and gentle encouragement with tugs at the lead failed. There was nothing else for it; he was dragged forcibly round the park. The Rottweiler pulled backwards, he stood stock still, he sat and he rolled onto his back – in whatever position, he was dragged bodily around the park. On the second circuit, just when the humans were totally exhausted, the dog gave up, stood up, shook the mud off and trotted along on his lead. Harsh treatment perhaps, but the owner's fault as he should never have allowed the dog to reach that weight without breaking the habit.

THE RECALL

This is the single most important exercise to teach. A dog that will not come back on command is out of control and a danger to other dogs, people, livestock and itself. He bounds over to other dogs on the lead and wars ensue. The other dog is probably on the lead for a good reason – either he's a fighter or maybe a bitch on heat – and a dog on a lead feels vulnerable and is more likely to fight. With a big dog, it is irresponsible to allow this lack of good behaviour. A big dog bearing down on a Yorkie or a child is terrifying not only to them, but also to the owner or parent. You may know your dog is friendly but they don't. The answer to the eternal statement 'he won't come back' is 'yes he will, train him'. There is no dog that cannot be trained to return on command.

The early stage of recall training appears on page 33 of the chapter Training in the Home, as this is where it must begin, from the moment you pick the puppy up. This present section, therefore, covers the follow-on from that – when you are able to take the dog out of doors for his training. If he is already coming to you on command in the home, you start with a large advantage; but don't expect it to work every time outside where there are lots of much more interesting things to sniff and look at.

Start somewhere safe like the middle of a big park. Attach a piece of cord or strong string 15ft (4.6m) long to his collar and remove the lead. Keep the cord loose. When he is about 10ft (3m) away, call his name followed by 'come' in a firm but inviting voice. Crouch down to welcome him. If he doesn't respond, give the cord a sharp tug and then release the pressure, saying the command. Keep this up until either he comes to you or, as a last resort, you have to haul him in. In the early stages, you can use titbits or a favourite toy as an inducement, but phase them out as quickly as possible.

When he's returning on command, drop the cord and let him venture further. If he won't come back you'll still be close enough to grab the cord or stand on it. Now remove the cord completely. During the walk, make sure that you recall him several times; make a fuss of him and then let him go again. But beware. If you only wait until you are ready to leave the park to recall him, he'll associate 'come' with the end of his walk and become disobedient.

At 5 months, start to increase the pressure on him. If you don't, he'll start to throw his weight around and by 12 months he'll be refusing to return. Now wait until he's sniffing something interesting. Roll the lead up in your hand. Call him. If he doesn't come back, throw the lead at him as hard as you can and repeat the command, now in a friendly voice. Always throw first and call second on the repeat – the other way round and you risk him being on the way back as the lead hits him. If this happens, he is naturally confused. Don't concern yourself that you might hurt him; you won't, and you're teaching him something that may later save his life. Dogs do not like sudden frights and the sudden arrival of the lead will startle him into believing that you can hit him from a distance. Immediately the lead has landed, call him in a friendly but firm voice. This is important, for if you use a scolding tone at this stage he's likely to run away from you.

Instead of the lead, you can throw a check chain or an old bunch of keys – anything metallic that rattles. In time, all you will have to do is rattle them and he will scurry back. Do, however, use old keys. One dog definitely smiled when his handler threw car keys at him and they disappeared down a drain.

Obedience in returning from an interesting sniff doesn't necessarily extend to obedience in returning from a good game with another dog, but it is the start of a successful recall when he doesn't really want to come.

Enlist the help of a friend with a dog. Let the dogs play, then recall yours (name, first, followed by 'come'). As before, use the lead/keys/chain if he ignores you. Keep practising, letting him have some time playing with the other dog in between recalls. Now go out on your own and watch for other dogs in the distance. As soon as you see your dog has noticed one, call him back, then praise him. Do it every time you see another dog, but occasionally let him go off and play with a new friend after he has been obedient.

As the puppy grows up, always recall him when he gets 40 to 50yds (37 to 46m) away from you. By doing this, he will learn that he will always be called back so he will start to automatically check the distance himself. This takes some time to achieve, but is very worthwhile.

Never allow him to relapse on the recall. Large breeds usually gain in arrogance as they grow and often behave badly in adolescence. If this happens, go back to basics.

THE SIT

A novice handler can unwittingly teach bad habits in the sit unless he or she has practised the manoeuvres until they become second nature. It really is worth first practising without the dog, by clipping the lead to something at roughly the height where the dog's neck would be.

Stand with the 'dog' on your left, as you will for heelwork, but now holding the lead at waist level in your right hand. Move onto your right foot and stop suddenly (Plate 7). Then lift the lead with your left hand (Plate 8) and at the same time bring your right hand (still holding the lead) under your left hand to grasp the lead close to the buckle. As you do this, you release the lead with your left hand, leaving it free to place on the dog's rump and push his rear down into the 'sit' (Plate 9). The right hand is still on the lead, close to the buckle. When you are reaching across with your right hand to grasp the lead near the buckle, practise bending your knees in the right position – with the right foot in front of the left foot. If you find it difficult to balance with one foot in front of the other, then halt with both feet together, but still bend your knees.

Plates 7–9: It is worthwhile first practising the sit manoeuvres without the dog, by clipping the lead to something at roughly the same height as the dog's neck would be

Training Outside

Practise many times without the dog by going back to the full extent of the lead, walking two paces forward, and carrying out the prescribed movements. Now try it with the dog (Plates 10, 11, 12). Timing is extremely important as the commands must be simultaneous with confident movements. So, as you halt, speak the command; but make it firm and accentuate the 't' of 'sit'. Do not speak the dog's name first, for example 'Rex, sit'; just 'sit' and not 'sit-sit-sit-sit'. Once should do, repeat only if necessary. The command must only be given as you halt and the movements must be immediate.

At 5 to 6 months your dog should learn this fairly quickly (as long as you have practised and know what you are doing). Practise with him until you can stop in the heelwork position, still holding the lead in your right hand, and he sits just on the spoken command of 'sit'.

Plates 10–12: Now practise with the dog

Plates 13–14: When the 'sit' command is given the lead must not be taut at any time

You are now ready to leave him in a controlled sit. Start to use the training lead (see page 58). With the dog at the sit on your left, unclip the lead to its longer length, give the command 'sit' and raise your right finger (ensuring he sees it) at the same time (Plate 13). Holding the lead in your left hand, sidestep to the right to the full extent of the lead, repeating 'sit' and a raised right finger if he looks like moving. Do not allow the lead to become taut, it must be loose at all times (Plate 14). Stay away for only around thirty seconds then sidestep back, repeating the command and signal if he indicates he's going to move. When you are back by his side, praise him gently; but if he goes to get up, stop him immediately with a firm 'sit'. He must learn to stay in the position until you tell him he may move.

Make him stay in the sit while you adjust the lead back to the former shorter length; on no account let him stand up because he was a good boy. Pause a while before setting off. You must vary the length of time you pause because if you do not he will learn to judge the time and set off on his own, which is not desirable at all.

If he gets up at any time during the exercise, grab him by the collar and put him back in the original spot, telling him he is a bad dog. Once there, put him back in the sit and do it again. You are aiming for a time when you can leave him and return without him standing up. When he stays in the sit until you are ready to move off, give the command 'heel'. Never, ever give up and let him move off or stand up when he wants to. After the command 'sit' the next step has to be you saying 'heel'.

Formal training on the lead (6 months onwards)

The light lead should now be permanently replaced with a training lead (see page 58). Formal training should be done in short sessions of 15 to 20 minutes twice a day, which is about as long as the dog should be expected to concentrate. With practice, you'll learn to recognise the signs of total boredom that he'll display (Amy used to bark and howl) and know when to stop. Remember, however, that you must make him finish the last exercise he was doing before letting him off to play or he will think that an expression of boredom is all it needs to achieve immediate freedom from work.

HEELWORK

For formal training the new lead is now permanently trans-ferred from the left hand to the right hand (Plate 15). Take the dog to the park on his lead (or into your garden if it is very large). Put him in the sit on your left side and fold the lead in your right hand so that when your hand is held in the correct position – belt high – it is just slack. Tuck your left arm in (Plate 16). Do not put your left hand on the lead.

Step off with your left foot, at the same time using the command 'heel'. You may also tap your left thigh with your left hand to encourage the dog on. He must walk close to your left side, on a loose lead. If he pulls away forward or to the side, put your left hand on the lead and give it a sharp jerk, saying 'heel'. When you do this, the lead must always be slack as the motion has to be a sharp tug, not a drag. If, therefore, he has pulled the lead taut, extend your arm quickly so the lead slackens, then jerk it back quickly before it has had time to go taut again. The jerk should be powerful enough to lift his front paws off the ground, not soft and floppy. Do not worry, you will not hurt his neck.

Now is the time to get the tone of voice right. This is very important with heelwork as eventually, with heel free, you will only have voice control to rely on. As you set off, the 'heel' is firm but friendly and encouraging. When you use it to correct him, because he is going off course, it has to be deep and scolding; but revert immediately to a friendly tone as he corrects himself.

Start to vary the pace – run or jog, then slow, then brisk. This variation helps to keep his interest and will be needed if you later decide to go on to competition work. When he is walking nicely in a straight line at your side on a loose lead (probably not the first lesson), progress to going around corners.

(pp 76–7) Plates 15–16: Heelwork

RIGHT TURN

Make sure the lead is loose, tap your left side to get your dog's attention and then stoop down as you go right, encouraging him round with 'heel, heel' as necessary (Plate 17). If he pulls away or goes off in the wrong direction, use a sharp tug on the lead (Plate 18). After completing the turn, walk briskly in a straight line, praising him. The stooping down and encouraging him round gives him a better idea of what you want him to do and is better than constant jerks which you will not be able to use later with heel free.

RIGHT ABOUT TURN

This involves turning backwards to where you came from, starting to the right. This is taught in the same way as the right turn, but as the dog has further to go, be patient and encourage him round slowly the first few times, allowing him time to collect himself before setting off again at a brisk pace.

Plates 17–18: At the right turn, if the dog pulls away or goes in the wrong direction, use a sharp tug on the lead

LEFT TURN

This one is fun because chances are you'll fall over the dog or tread on him unless you practise the footwork first without him.

Walk forward and halt momentarily as your left foot comes forward. Pivot on the ball of the left foot, swinging your right side round across the path of the dog. At the same time, put your left hand on the lead and check his forward movement (Plate 19). Done properly, he will come with you and you can step off again briskly, praising him. A crucial part is to ensure that he is not in front of you when you start the movement.

Plate 19: The left turn manoeuvre

TEACHING THE ADULT DOG TO HEEL

The basics of training an adult dog (or one 10 to 12 months plus) are the same, but if a check chain (see page 60) is used with the training lead, more pressure can be applied and results expected more quickly. The best chain is the long link chain shown. The small link chains are not as good and, indeed, if a dog will respond to a small link chain he doesn't need one and a leather collar would be equally as good.

It is worth repeating that check chains are not choke chains as they are often wrongly called. They are not used to choke a dog, but to check – a short, sharp movement. A check chain also has to be put on correctly or it will not release and the dog *will* be choked. The illustration (page 61) shows the correct method. With the adult dog, a certain amount of physical strength is needed, but with the right techniques most healthy adults can manage.

Walk off with the dog at your left, holding the lead as described in the earlier heelwork section. He will probably start to get ahead of you. As his rear legs come level with your legs:

- Halt with your left foot forward.
- Put your left hand on the lead immediately in front of the right hand (Plate 20).
- Extend both arms forward and move your body forward by bending the left knee but keeping the left foot on the ground for balance and the right leg straight. This will make the lead go loose (Plate 21).
- Jerk the lead sharply backwards, pulling your arms into your sides, at the same time bringing your left leg back to your right leg, and straighten your body. Say 'heel' sharply as you do it (Plate 22).
- Immediately he is back at your side, take your left hand off the lead, tuck it back in and walk on.

Plate 20

(pp 84–5) Plates 21–22

Training Outside

This sounds complicated as it all has to happen very quickly and smoothly, but with practice it isn't. It's designed to use your whole body weight rather than arm strength and is, in fact, often the only method a female handler can use with a large, untrained adult dog.

To do this properly you must dispel any misgivings you have about hurting the dog. The hardest jerk a strong man can give will not cause pain. If the dog yips, it will be through fright, not hurt, and this is exactly what you need to get him under proper control.

Keep practising until he heels properly and then progress to the other movements described.

THE DOWN

The down is an exercise that can save a dog's life. In some respects, it's even more important than instant recall, as you may find the dog in a position of danger away from you across a road, or with a car approaching. Teaching him to drop immediately on command and wait for you to get to him is, in these circumstances, more useful than the ability to call him back.

The down is a supressive movement and, as such, must be taught sensitively to a young dog (never before 6 months old) in order not to frighten him. Forget any of the strange methods taught in some dog schools as many of these are known to make a dog nervous. For example, some schools teach the dog to sit first and then they pull his front legs away. Not only is this disconcerting for the dog, but you'll probably end up with him always sitting first before he goes down. This is slow, sloppy and not something to teach if you ever want him to drop on command. Other schools teach you to put your foot on the lead and drag him down by the neck. With most dogs, this makes them very nervous and fearful of the exercise.

There are two good methods for teaching the down. Always start with the first method as it is usually effective; progress to the second only if the first fails or if the dog is adult and you need a different technique to handle his bulk.

Start with the dog at heel in the usual position, with the lead in your right hand. As you halt smartly, put your left hand on his neck, in front of the shoulder blades (Plate 23, page 88). Your hand must be cupped in a 'C' as shown (Plate 24, page 89). Bring your right hand across your body so that the lead is loose, say 'down' harshly and at the same time apply pressure backwards and downwards with the left hand (Plate 25, page 90). The dog should fold downwards, front end first. Make sure that your left hand is far enough forward; if it is over his shoulder blades you have no chance of getting him down.

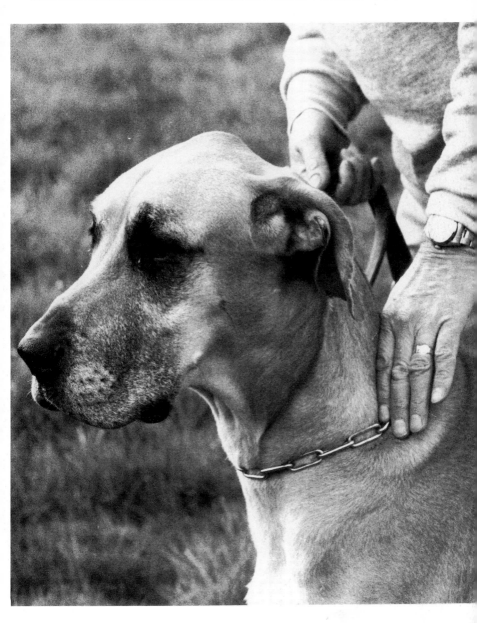

(pp 88–90) *Plates 23–25: Teaching the 'down'*

Some dogs learn this quickly, others are a problem. For instance he may shift smartly sideways to avoid your hand on his neck. If this happens, keep the lead taut in your right hand to stop him sidestepping and bend down with him, not loosening the lead until he is down (Plate 26, page 92). The other trick some develop is to roll over on their back in submission at the harsh command. With one of these tricksters, keep your left foot against his right side as he goes down to stop him rolling towards you, and after he is down, move your left hand quickly from his neck to his left side to stop him going over that way (Plate 27, page 93). When he is steady, slowly release the pressure of your hand and repeat 'down', standing upright as you do. Keep going until he will stay down and allow you to stand upright beside him.

As with any of the exercises, never allow the dog to get up when he chooses to. If it takes all day, you must not give up until he is in the down up to the very minute you say 'heel' and start to walk.

The second method, as already mentioned, is for particularly stubborn or very large/strong dogs that don't respond to the basic method. Amy had to be trained in the down in this way as she was immensely strong and stubborn about the exercise. If you have to resort to this, first practise it without the dog, with the lead clipped to something static at roughly his head height, as timing and a smooth movement are very important.

Walk in the normal heelwork position and stop suddenly with your right foot in front of the left (mid-stride), then pivot left to face the side of the dog (Plate 28, page 94). Drop the lead and immediately use both cupped hands on his neck to push him down, using your body weight and a harsh 'down' (Plates 29, 30, page 94, 95). As in the previous method, push backwards and down at the same time.

Plates 26–27: Some dogs learn the 'down' quickly, others may need extra help

Plates 28–30: For the particularly stubborn or very large dogs the second method may have to be used

THE STAY

This is one of the most difficult of the basic training methods to teach, as a mistake in tone of voice will make the dog sit or go down. Remember, 'sit' is firm and sharp, but in a normal voice; 'down' is very firm and slightly threatening. The tone of voice needed for 'stay' is like that used for 'sit', but more friendly and gentle, with a hint of warning!

Walk on normally, halt, then lower and loosen the lead in front of the dog (Plate 31). Starting just behind the front left leg, run your left hand gently along his side, finishing by holding his left rear thigh, saying 'stay' as you do. The reason for the smoothing movement is reassurance, and ending up holding his thigh prevents him from sitting. Whatever you do, do not

tower over him threateningly or he will go down instead.

If he tries to pip you to the post every time by either sitting or going down immediately you halt, get him used to your hand along his back and side as you walk. If you still have difficulty, or suspect you aren't handling the lead properly, drop it completely and use both hands (Plate 32).

Whichever method you have used, once you are sure he is steady, release your hand(s) slowly, still saying 'stay' gently and with warning, and show him the flat of your right hand (Plate 33, pages 98–9). Keep practising until he will 'stay' and not move off, sit or lie down without your command.

Plates 31–32: One of the most difficult of the basic training methods is the 'stay'

Plate 33: Show him the flat of your right hand

RECALL – THE ADULT DOG

Taking on an adult, untrained, large-breed dog is not easy, but training is possible. First read the section on recall in the early training section (page 65). For the first week, keep him on the lead when outside and just practise recall as for a puppy, in the home or garden. Buy a check chain in case you find he's too strong to control on a leather collar, but keep it in your pocket as a last resort. During the week you are keeping him on the lead, start the recall outside. Extend the training lead and let it go loose (Plate 34). Before he is far enough away for it to tighten, call him to you. If he doesn't respond, repeat the command accompanied by a sharp tug on the lead.

When the week is up, go to the park armed with 13yd (12m) of the lightest very strong cord you can find, and a bunch of old keys or spare check chain. Proceed exactly as for the stage of training the young dog on the cord, but throw the metallic object at him if he disobeys, rather than tug the cord. Remember always to call his name first, followed by 'come'. If he doesn't react, throw the object first and then repeat his name and the command. Crouch down as he comes to you (Plate 35) so he knows that, although he's been punished, it's safe to come to you – you're friendly again. Make a fuss of him and then let him go off to play. You'll know when the time is right to remove the cord and when you can trust him.

POINTS TO REMEMBER

- Do not keep repeating the command as he comes towards you unless he deviates.
- Make a fuss of him before going to hunt for the keys or chain that you threw.
- Stand still; don't go towards him or move until he's right back with you.
- Don't praise him until he's right back. If you start when he's a few feet away, he'll think the exercise is finished and dash off again.

Plates 34–35: With the dog still on the lead begin teaching the 'recall'

Off the lead

When the dog is steady and obedient on the lead, you can progress to off-lead work, which is very satisfying for both you and your dog.

HEEL FREE

Take a toy out with you to get him back in case you experience real difficulty, but use it only as a last resort. It is most unlikely that you will need it if you progress to off-lead work when your dog is truly ready.

In a safe, secluded place, walk briskly with him on the lead and, without pausing, click the lead clip but do not remove it. He may think the lead has been removed and pull away. If so, correct him and say 'heel'. He must get used to the click of the clip and not associate it with immediate freedom to play – what you are doing is making him always unsure as to whether he is on the lead or not.

Make him sit. Unclip the lead quietly and just slip it under his collar by about 3in (76mm). Your own manner must now be totally confident, as he will sense it if you are not, and may misbehave. Using a normal tone of voice, say 'heel' and start off. After about twenty paces, pull the lead from under the collar and dangle it close to his neck so that it jangles and he thinks he is still on the lead. The reason for the different voice tones for 'heel' now becomes obvious. If he tries to forge ahead (Plate 36) use the stern, scolding 'heel' with gentle praise when he drops back. Be careful about the level of praise as too much will make him think that work is over and he can go off and play. If he starts to play up, put him back on the lead for a short, sharp lesson and then try again. If he drops back during heel free, encourage him on gently by patting your left leg and saying 'heel' in an encouraging voice (Plate 37, page 104). The correct position is shown in Plate 38, page 105.

Plate 36

Training Outside

Plates 37–8: When the dog is obedient on the lead you can progress to off-lead work

Training Outside

Some dogs progress easily from heel on the lead to heel free but others do not. If you have real difficulty, try using two leads at once – a light nylon one added to his heavier training one. Clip both leads to the collar (Plate 39) and walk for around 50yd (46m) so that he gets used to the weight. Make him sit. Hold the nylon lead back out of view (Plate 40) and loose while you make a big thing of removing the training lead and dropping it on the ground where he can see it. Holding the nylon lead in your left hand, step off straightaway (Plate 41) and he will think that the reduced weight means he has no lead clipped to his collar. If he plays up, check him as usual. Eventually he will believe that he is never without a lead and will behave when you remove both.

Plates 39–41: If the dog does not progress easily from heel on the lead to heel free, try using two leads at once

Plate 40

Plate 41

SIT

With the dog on the lead, put him into the sit and drop the lead. As before, sidestep away, but now move in a semi-circle around the front of him. If he moves, repeat the hand signal and command (Plate 42). Eventually, remove the lead and take it with you, keeping it rolled up to throw at him if he moves and ignores a repeated command and hand signal.

- Watch your tone of voice. Too harsh a 'sit' and he'll go down instead.
- Make sure the lead is loose before you drop it.
- Don't use an extra command eg 'sit, stay'.
- Always use the hand signal with the command. Soon he'll respond to that alone, if that is what you wish.

DOWN

Being able to put the dog into the down and leave him isn't taught so that the owner can go into a shop and leave the dog down outside. No large dog, however well trained, should ever be left unattended where there is any traffic or while there are strangers around.

As you have been practising, walk him heel free and then put him in the down. Push his hips over to one side (Plate 43). In this position, the dog is relaxed and not tensed for flight. Step sideways away from him, point to the floor, repeating 'down' (Plate 44). Go about 8ft (2.4m), then sidestep back. At no time must he get up until you are back at his side, have said 'heel' and moved off. When you are moving, now is the time to praise him gently.

Plates 43–44: When the dog is in the 'down' position step backwards away from the dog

Progressively increase the distance from him and go on to do a semi-circle in front of him at a distance of around 30ft (9m). When he stays steady for at least five minutes at a time, start going out of sight for a minute. Choose a place (behind undergrowth for instance) where you can see him but he can't see you. If he starts to move, shout the command. The first few times you may find yourself on your back in a thicket looking at the sky with a large puppy on your chest saying 'Found you, aren't I clever?' Do not laugh; be stern with him. Drag him back to exactly the same spot you left him in and do it all over again until he will let you out of sight.

You're now ready for the real lifesaver – the emergency down when the dog should drop immediately to the ground, no matter where he is or how far away from you as long as he is in earshot. Put him back on the lead and jog with him. Stop suddenly and tower over him with your right hand in the position illustrated (Plate 45). At the same time, say 'down' threateningly. Your movements must be fast and concise if he is to respond with the necessary speed.

Now unclip the lead to its full extent (Plate 46) and, with him standing, move round in front. You now have to get the dog to go down in front of you, so as you give the 'down' command, move your right foot forward and place your right hand on the lead close to the collar (Plate 47) and pull him down. When he

Plates 45–47: Teaching the emergency down

is down, move your right leg backwards and stand in front of him. Call him to you, using his name, followed by 'come'. As he does so, move forward aggressively, point down and say 'down' (Plate 48). If he fails to go down immediately, step towards him and put him in the down as before. Practise until his reaction is immediate. However, don't do this every time you recall him or he will come very slowly, trying to second-guess when you'll say 'down'. Now progress to moving further away with the lead dropped before calling him, then take the lead off completely. If you have problems, it will be because you moved on from the first step (jogging) too fast. Go back and start again.

At the stage where he drops smartly, start making him do the exercise at odd times, for example when he is running around playing and distracted. Have the loose check chain or keys with you to throw at him should he ignore the command. With practice, you will be able to shout 'down', pointing to the floor and the dog will flatten to the ground immediately. If,

therefore, he is ever in a position of danger, you can drop him and he'll stay still until you get to him.

For two reasons, the dog must not anticipate a recall from the down, therefore you must always go to him after putting him in the down. First, you may want to progress to distance control work where you can move the dog by hand signals from any one of the positions to any other – from the down to the sit, the sit to the stand etc. If you always recall after the down he'll automatically bound towards you instead of waiting for the next signal.

The second reason is safety. If you have dropped him because a tractor is coming into the field, you don't want him to move until you're at his side with the lead. If you always recall him from the down he may well misread your movements as you approach him and think you are recalling, as that is what you will have programmed him to expect.

Plate 48: When the dog is in the 'down' position call him to you, followed immediately by 'down'

STAY

On the lead, put the dog into the stand with the command 'stay'. Extend the lead and move sideways, showing the dog the flat of your hand and repeating 'stay' (Plate 49). Move back into him and walk off before praising him. Extend the distance by dropping the lead first (Plate 50, pages 118–19), then progress by moving round the front of him in a semi-circle. At any sign of movement, give the command and hand signal. When you think he is ready, progress to removing the lead.

Be careful that you don't confuse him by tone of voice. 'Sit' and 'stay' can sound very similar, but 'sit' is short and sharp with the 't' extended and 'stay' must be softer and drawn out. If you have a particularly bright and responsive dog, he may not let you get further than the 's' before he sits down. If this happens, just use the 'ay' which is harder to confuse, and bring in the beginning of the word later.

Plate 49: When the dog is on the lead give the command 'stay'

GENERAL COMMENTS

● Vary the sequence of exercises and the time you leave him in each position. If you don't, he'll start to second-guess you, and move automatically to what he thinks is next.

● Don't push too hard for too long or he will become bored and resentful. Sessions of 15 to 20 minutes are normally long enough, but watch him in case his boredom level is lower.

● Always make the dog finish the last exercise. If he starts to play up through boredom, he still has to complete what you last asked him to do, even if it takes another 20 minutes.

Plate 50: Extend the distance by dropping the lead, and move sideways

5 Kennelling and Boarding

Outdoor kennelling

Both short- and long-haired dogs can be safely kennelled out of doors if you have room and you choose to do so. Contrary to the beliefs of some, it is not cruel to kennel a puppy outdoors at the times you would normally leave him alone, he's as happy in his kennel as in the kitchen. The only time it becomes cruel is if the kennel is used constantly and the dog does not have sufficient human contact. If the kennel is used only at those times when the dog would otherwise have been left in the kitchen or house, it can actually be kinder. Outside, he has his run so that he can relieve himself if he's uncomfortable, sniff the air and listen to the natural sounds around him. It also means that your furniture and carpets will survive his puppy-hood, but this is just a secondary bonus.

Kennels can be of brick or wooden construction and must be draughtfree and waterproof but well ventilated. The sleeping area must be of a size that the dog can move around and stand up comfortably, so a kennel large enough for a pointer would be too small for a wolfhound. It should be sited as close as possible to the house – not the end of the garden – so that the puppy feels he is not far away from you. In the sleeping quarters provide old carpet or a bean bag (never straw). Attached to the kennel should be a run of a minimum of 10ft (3m), longer if space is available.

If you intend to kennel your dog outside, do it immediately, from the first night. He has probably come straight from a kennel so is already used to the idea that that is where he sleeps. Don't think you're being kind by letting him sleep indoors for the first few nights – it's cruel. He just begins to

Kennelling and Boarding

settle, is removed to another environment and naturally becomes confused and unhappy.

Take a blanket with you when you go to pick him up and do it as early as possible in the day. When you get home, put the blanket in the kennel and see if he will go in on his own to explore. Do not, under any circumstances, close the door at this stage. If he isn't interested, go in yourself and entice him in to play, praising him all the time. Feed him in his run, close to the kennel door, and make sure there is always plenty of fresh water in there. Stay with him as much as you can and allow him to play in and around the kennel all day without shutting the door. At night, give him his last feed, check his water and close him in. You may be lucky and have a quiet night, but you probably won't. If he howls or barks, take no notice for an hour and then go out. Do not open the door, just shout 'kennel' at him in a firm voice. If he doesn't scuttle back in, go in and place him on his blanket repeating 'kennel'. Use no affection or cuddles. Watch for a minute and, if he scrambles out again, push him back in with the command. Keep the procedure up all night if need be, leaving him each time for as long as your nerves will hold up.

If he keeps it up for many nights, check the size of his run. If it is too small he will be unhappy and trying to explore further. Never chain him in his kennel; such confinement is both cruel and unnecessary.

Taking on an adult dog that is used to sleeping indoors is more difficult. The methods used to settle him and chastise him are the same, but you can afford to be much firmer than with a puppy. If he doesn't settle, try throwing a check chain at the kennel from an upper window while he is at his noisiest. It should startle him into silence as he won't know where it's come from and will think you're lurking around invisibly. If after a week he hasn't settled, the chances are he never will and you'll simply have to give up and let him sleep indoors.

There are manufacturers that specialise in building kennels, but if you are good at DIY you might like to build one yourself.

Plan 2 – outdoor kennel (German Shepherd size)

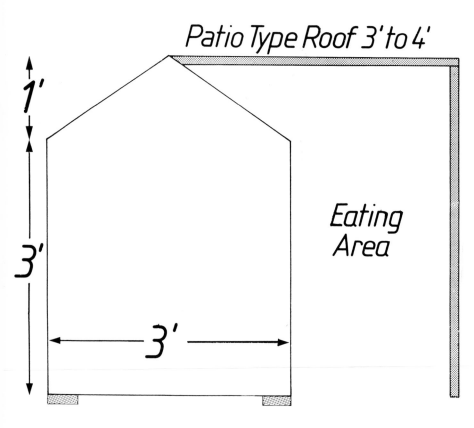

Patio Type Roof 3' to 4'

1'

3'

3'

Eating Area

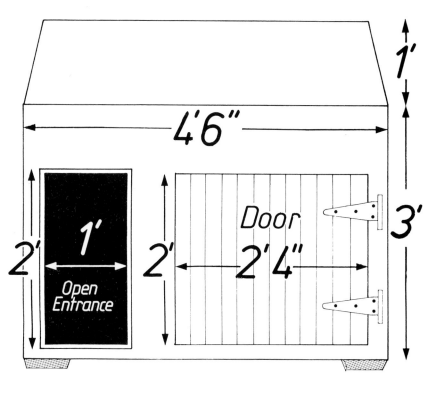

Plan 2 shows a kennel of a size suitable for a German Shepherd. When Hobson arrived he took over such a kennel from Prangen who moved into the house permanently on retirement. Note the covered 'patio' section where the dog can eat his food in all weathers without getting wet.

Boarding the large dog

Just because you have a dog, you shouldn't change your lifestyle and forgo holidays abroad. One option is to leave the dog with friends who are willing to take this on, but, with a large dog, it really is a heavy responsibility to confer on anyone. The better way is to leave the dog in the care of one of the very good boarding kennels. At some time, everyone hears horror stories about kennels and, while these may be justified in some instances, often people are simply 'horrified' at conditions totally suitable for a dog but not right by 'human standards'. If you choose kennels carefully in the first instance and then always use the same one, the staff will soon come to know the dog and he'll be pleased to see them.

A personal recommendation from a friend is a good start, but do not visit only that one kennel. Kennels suitable for smaller breeds do not always have the correct set-up for larger ones; so if your friend has a Cocker Spaniel, the kennels he recommends may have facilities too small for the comfort of your St Bernard. Go and see at least three kennels and inspect them all in the same manner.

First ring to make an appointment at a time that suits the kennels. It isn't clever to surprise them to find out how they operate when no one is looking because you'll probably arrive when they are in the middle of feeding time, or just when everything is quiet and you'll start all the dogs barking. Ask them if they take a dog like yours. Some kennels will not take certain breeds like Danes if they have had previous bad experience in settling them. Ask them also whether the kennels are heated. In winter a dog that usually sleeps indoors must have a heated kennel. Enquire when you can come to see the kennels. Make it plain that you actually want to see the sleeping quarters. Never consider a kennel where they will not allow you to see the conditions the dogs are kept in.

When you arrive, look at the size of the sleeping quarters. There must be sufficient room for the dog to turn comfortably and enough head-room in case he decides to put his paws up on the wire or walls. Some kennels have overhead heating lamps that look a bit like lights. These are fine, but in some kennels they are too low for the safety of larger breeds, so check carefully. Assess the general cleanliness of the place. One 'heap' in a dog's toilet area is all right but several show that it hasn't been cleaned for some time. Check whether all the pens have clean water.

Eye up the condition of the dogs. One or two may look sad and a bit out of condition but it may not be the kennels' fault. Ask: it may be that the dog is a rescue one, or simply that he has been in for a long time and is the pining type. Notice whether there are other large dogs there. Some kennels populated entirely with lap dogs will stoutly maintain that they can manage your Rottweiler. Be very sceptical.

Boarding premises vary enormously in layout. Some of them are arranged as separate kennels, each with its own concrete run. Others, like the one the Danes go to, have separate exercise areas some way from the kennels themselves. They maintain that it is the only way of guaranteeing that each dog has personal, human contact, as the kennel maids have to go in to get them, put their leads and collars on, and walk them to the exercise area. It makes a great deal of sense and gives the dog a feeling of comfortable routine. If the kennel is arranged like this, check carefully that there isn't only one exercise area for a lot of dogs. Kennels rarely put dogs in together for fear of fighting, so if there are fourteen dogs and

Kennelling and Boarding

one run, logic says your dog is unlikely to get more than half an hour a day out there, if that. However, the individual run is fine as long as it is at least 10ft (3m) long.

Try to remember that you aren't looking at a hotel for yourself. The better kennels are fairly stark places and look a bit like Alcatraz. But if these stark kennels fulfil all the criteria above, you can leave your dog confident that it will be catered for properly, and the presence of other large breeds shows that they know how to handle them. Avoid the 'luxury' dog hotels that are sadly popping up. The majority of these are run by people only out to make money and your dog would much prefer to be with real 'doggie' people and have lots of time in a big run rather than a feather mattress and bedside lamp.

Even if you aren't going away, make sure that you put your dog into kennels for a long weekend at least twice in the first year that you have him. This accustoms him to being left there and gives you confidence in that you can always go and get him if they ring you. If the first time you leave him you disappear for a fortnight, he may think he's been dumped and suffer as a result.

Many kennels will allow you to take in the dog's bed, but most will not allow bean bags as many dogs tear their beds up in annoyance at being left. Anyone who has ever experienced a burst bean bag will appreciate their point – polystyrene beads are almost impossible to pick up. So, if your dog normally sleeps on a bean bag, cover it with a blanket for a few days before he goes into kennels, and take the blanket in with him.

No matter how good the kennels is, many dogs lose weight and condition through stress. Some also bark so much at the sight of other dogs that they lose their bark. This will return in a few weeks and isn't a matter for concern. All kennels will call a vet if they are worried about a dog, so this should reassure you. You are presented with the vet's fee on your return and should pay it cheerfully; it proves they were doing their job well.

One last point. Do not forget to take the dog's vaccination certificate with you as the kennels will wish to see he has been vaccinated and had his annual boosters. If they don't ask for the certificates, be very wary about leaving the dog as they aren't ensuring that killer diseases are not brought in.

6 Fighters and Chasers

Natural and other fighters

Some dogs are born fighters – Hobson is. He loves Prangen, the old retired Weimeraner, but will fight any other dog that comes up to him. You'll probably be hoping that this chapter will tell you what to do to stop a natural fighter. Unfortunately, it can only offer advice that may work with some dogs, not all.

Prevention is always better than cure, so start off correctly by allowing your young puppy to mix frequently with other dogs of tried, stable temperament. A fright as a puppy, if another dog attacks, can turn a dog into a fighter on the principle of bite before you are bitten. Keep him away from other dogs on leads as these feel vulnerable and are more likely to snap. Dog-training schools are a good place for him to socialise and get used to being around other dogs.

In natural fighters, you'll see indications before a year old. A dog squaring up for a fight will stand as if on tip toe, tail high and rigid and maybe put his head over the neck of the other dog. If this happens, do not go towards him as he'll think 'great – here's reinforcements' and dive in. Jog away from him, calling in a nice voice something like 'come on, silly' and hope that when he sees his back-up disappearing he'll come after you. If this doesn't work and a fight ensues, you must break it up immediately. A well-trained dog will often break off solely on a screamed command of 'leave', so try this first. If it fails, you have no option but to resort to violence before one of them is badly injured. Hit them with the lead or a shoe, or kick them hard. Never put your hand in to pull them apart or you will surely be bitten. At this stage, your own dog will bite you. It isn't deliberate, it's just that he'll bite anything in the way without stopping to wonder what it is. If there's a bucket of water or a hose handy, douse them immediately.

A dog on a lead is definitely more likely to fight than one free. He feels restricted by the lead, at a disadvantage, and also feels that he has your back-up. If he growls at another passing dog, or makes a lunge, check him hard on the check chain saying 'no' firmly. You have to try to get to the stage where he is more worried about the punishment from you than he is about the other dog. This kind of handling will work on all but the true pack-leader type. With this temperament you may be able to improve behaviour, but you will never eradicate its nature completely. Such an attitude is just acceptable in a working dog like Hobson, who can be prevented from fighting by dominance and training. It is not acceptable in a large pet who could easily kill another dog. If you have this situation you would be well advised to rehouse the dog somewhere more suitable before it does any damage.

It is often said that a dog will not fight a bitch. Most husbands don't beat their wives, but some do and some dogs will fight a bitch! Even pacifist dogs hold grudges against other specific dogs who have attacked them, and will never forget the offender. At 2 years, Amy was playing with a German Shepherd bitch who attacked her. Not being the type to retire quietly, Amy fought back. Luckily, she came on a screamed 'leave' and the incident was forgotten. A year later, walking quietly on her lead in a busy shopping area, she suddenly rounded a corner to come face to face with the German Shepherd. With the speed of light, before anything could be done, she launched herself at the other bitch and tossed her 4ft (1m) in the air. By then, she was back under control and, luckily the other bitch was only winded. Amy walked arrogantly on, with her nose in the air and an expression that said 'got my own back'. She will never forget that particular bitch and will always go for her in future. So if your dog has a similar experience, try to avoid the offender and always watch for the other dog in the distance.

Curing chasing

It is a natural instinct for a dog to chase a fast-moving object, but in the human world this usually means joggers, motor-cyclists and cars and presents a real danger that must be stopped. Jogging innocently through the park, it's bad enough to have a terrier snapping at your heels, but a 10st (63kg) mastiff thundering after you is really terrifying.

If you have managed to achieve instant recall, you need read no further as you can simply watch for joggers etc and call the dog back to heel as soon as you see one in the distance. If you cannot rely upon instant recall, you will have to enlist the help of a jogging friend. Take a spare check chain or old keys with you and meet at the local park. Give the chain to the friend and ask him to jog off. Release the dog. When he is thundering after your friend, and is about 20ft (6m) behind him, get the friend to turn suddenly and throw the object hard at the dog, shouting 'no' at the same time. The dog will be so startled that it is unlikely he will ever chase joggers again. The same method can be used with dogs that chase motorcycles or horses.

Alternatively, you can attach the dog to a length of strong cord about 20ft (6m) long. Start with a leather collar and only progress to a check chain if that does not work. When he takes off after the object, shout 'no' and jerk him back sharply with the cord. In full flight, this will give him quite a shock and may even cure him first time. If not, keep going until he is cured.

Horse riders are so often in danger from unruly dogs scaring their mounts, that most will be quite happy to co-operate. Ask a rider if he or she minds if you show the horse to the dog. Make sure the dog is on a check chain and make him sit by your side and look at the horse while you talk to the rider. At any sign of excitement or movement towards the horse, check him sharply and say 'no'. In time he'll come to get used to horses and will learn that they are just another thing that must not be touched or chased.

There is no need to train a dog not to chase farm animals as no dog (apart from the farmer's own) should be anywhere near farm animals without being on a lead. Dogs worrying livestock are likely to be shot by the farmer. This is quite understandable – his livelihood is at stake.

7 Visiting the Vet

A very large dog that is afraid of the vet, or refuses to be examined, is a danger to the vet and itself, as it may not be possible for the vet to carry out a sufficiently thorough examination without being bitten.

Visits to the vet need not be traumatic experiences for either you or the dog if you accustom him to the kind of procedures that will take place. Basically, it's logic. If no one had ever grabbed your rear end before, you'd jump out of your skin the first time someone did, and in future would try to avoid the place where it happened! He must get used to all types of examination procedure from opening his mouth without struggling, to having his feet lifted for claw-clipping. When he is young, carry out the following with him two or three times a week:

- Lift him onto a table. Stand facing his right side, put your left arm under him, just behind his back legs and your right arm between his front legs (Plates 51, 52). This gives you a firm hold and means you will not frighten him by dropping him or letting him slip. When he's up, speak reassuringly, telling him he's a good boy. It's important that you enlist the help of friends, getting them to lift him onto the table occasionally, in order that he is not afraid if a stranger (the vet) ever has to do it for you. But ensure that you show them how to lift him as it could do more harm than good if a stranger lets him slip and makes him nervous. Eventually, a very large dog will have to be examined on the floor, as he will be too heavy to lift. But it is still worth getting him used to the lifting procedure as it will be useful at the surgery when he is young and will, anyway, get him used to being manhandled.
- Look in his ears and clean them gently with cotton wool dipped in warm water and squeezed out. Be careful not to probe beyond the part of the ear that you can see.
- Also with cotton wool, swab his eyes.
- Run your hands all over him, kneading his stomach gently.

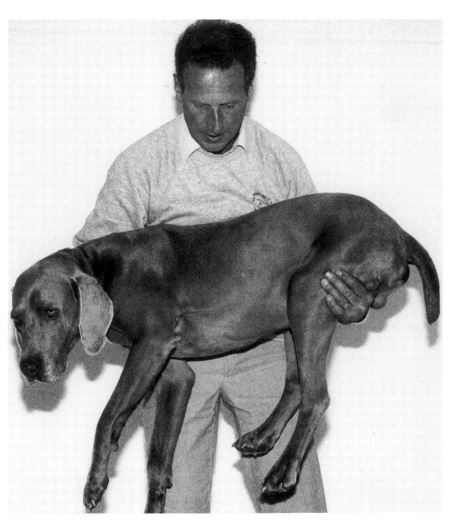

Plate 51: Lifting the dog onto the table for inspection

133

Plate 52: Correct position of hands for lifting the dog

- Lift his tail and firmly (but not hard) squeeze his rear end with your other hand. This will prepare him for the thermometer and go some way towards preparing him for the unpleasant sensation of having his anal gland evacuated if it becomes necessary.
- Open his mouth and inspect his teeth. Put a vitamin pill as far back in his mouth towards his throat as you can reach, close his mouth and stroke his throat until he swallows (Plate 53). If you do this now, you won't have trouble later getting him to take medicines. Don't assume that this is unnecessary because you can always mix the medicine with food. A very sick dog will often refuse food but still find the strength to clench his teeth firmly if you haven't taught him to open his mouth when you want him to.
- Lift his feet in turn and examine the pads. When he is young, clip his claws yourself with proper dog-claw clippers, but ensure that you remove only the very tip as you'll hurt him if you cut lower into the quick. However, a fully grown, very large dog has immensely strong claws that can only be clipped using an instrument that looks like a pair of pruning shears. This is best done by the vet who knows exactly what he is doing and how far down to cut.

Enlist the help of friends to run through the procedures for you. They may baulk at the rear end, but as long as the dog gets used to strangers carrying out all the other examinations, the rear end doesn't matter.

Vets despair at the inability of most people to hold their dogs properly while the examination is in progress. You'll be extremely popular if you demonstrate that you know exactly how to help by holding the dog correctly. For a general examination, first make sure the dog is wearing a good-fitting leather collar that he can't back out of. Facing him, put both

Plate 53: Giving the dog a vitamin pill, stroking his throat until he swallows

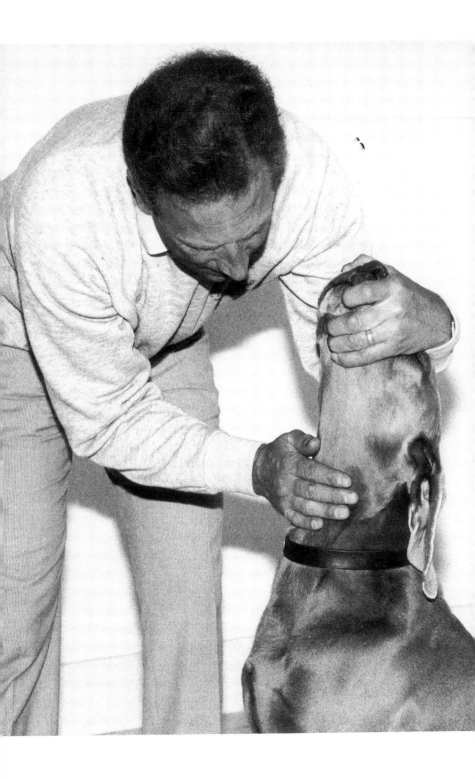

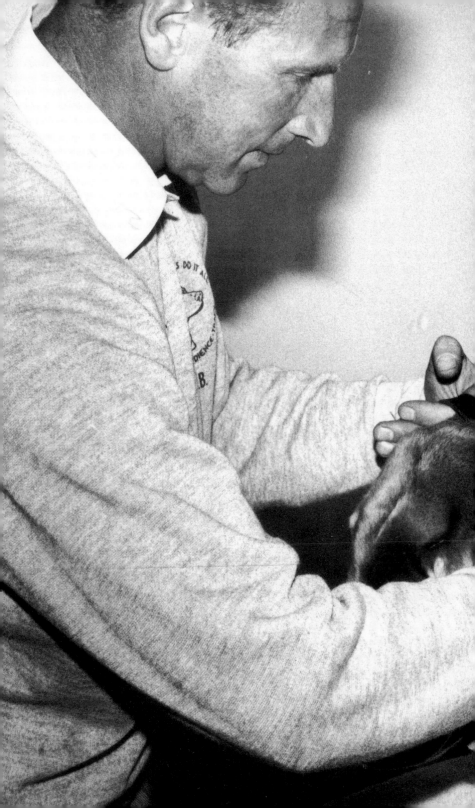

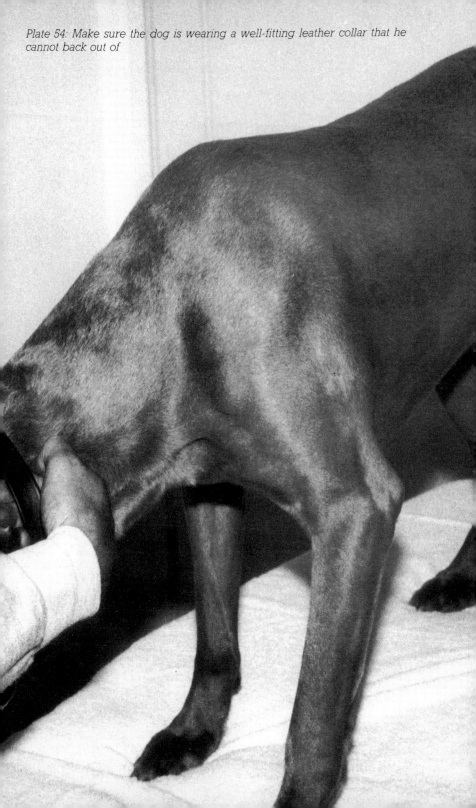

Plate 54: Make sure the dog is wearing a well-fitting leather collar that he cannot back out of

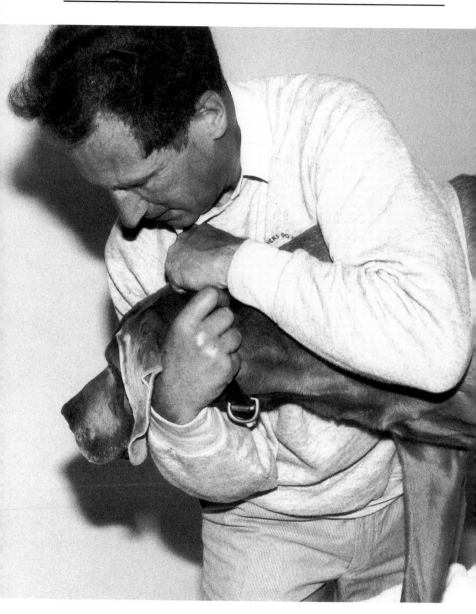

Plate 55: Hold the dog firmly to prevent him biting the vet

hands underneath the collar from the back with arms parallel to his muzzle (Plate 54). In this position, it's very difficult for him to turn round and bite the vet. Talk to him reassuringly as the examination progresses. Many dogs hate having their claws clipped and need to be held very firmly. Facing the dog's left or right side, bend over and clasp him round the neck in a good imitation of a wrestling hold (Plate 55). If you hold him very firmly to you, he won't be able to bite the vet (or you).

Summary

Those who have never trained a large dog before may think some of the training in this book is harsh. You must remember that the dog is first and foremost a pack animal. You take him into your pack, show him firmly how he must behave and he will automatically look to you for leadership. Knowing his place in the pack is a comfort to him as dogs like to know their own position in the hierarchy.

If you do not establish dominance over any dog, large or small, when it is young, it will try to dominate you and become pack leader itself. Such dogs are dangerous as they demonstrate their leadership by bullying humans and animals, going as far as to bite to make another submit. In the pack situation, the dog that stepped out of line would be punished by the pack leader in more serious ways than any you are likely to use with your voice and a check chain.

In training, you simply go as far as is necessary to gain his respect for you. It's a sensitive balance that will become obvious to you as you train your own dog. Dogs do have different personalities and different levels of wishing to please. Some will respond eagerly and quickly, while others will fight you for dominance. Start gently but firmly and only increase pressure if it is obvious that it's the only way your dog will respond. All the time you are training him, keep one thought at the front of your mind. He is going to be a big, heavy animal that could be dangerous. If you allow this to happen you will have to get rid of him and deprive him of the one thing he loves most in the world – you.

Train him with love and patience and you'll have the best friend you could wish for.

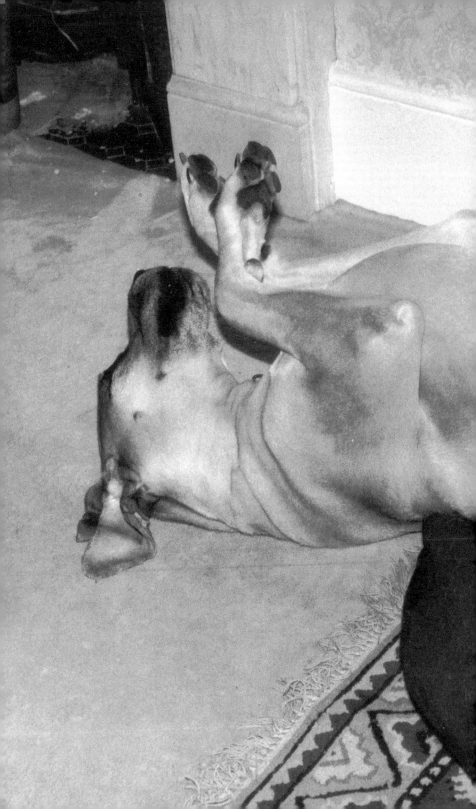

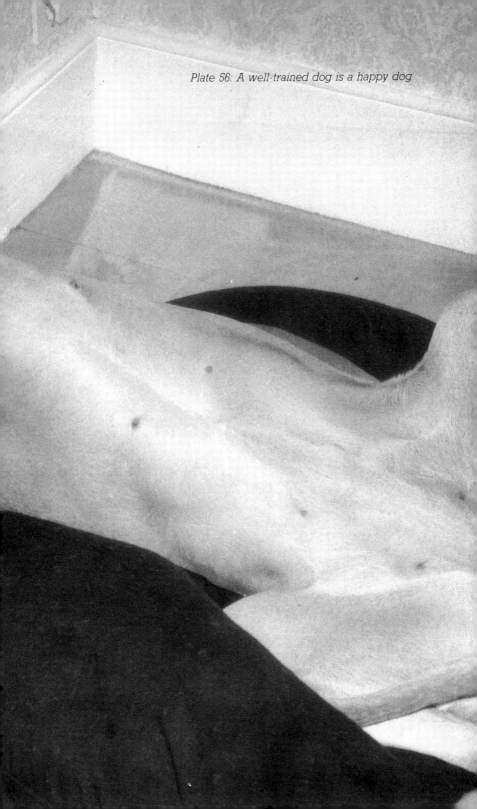

Plate 56: A well-trained dog is a happy dog

About the Authors

Paul Dodd

Paul Dodd has been a London Metropolitan Police dog handler since 1970, when he was given the force's first Weimeraner puppy, Monroes Thor, to train. Determined to prove the worth of Weimeraners in police work, Paul and Thor collected numerous cups and certificates in working trials, with Thor becoming the first Weimeraner to gain the Kennel Club qualifications of 'working dog excellent' and 'police dog excellent'. As members of the central demonstration team, Paul and Thor appeared at Crufts, Wembley and the Royal Tournament. Before Thor's retirement in 1980 he became a TV celebrity, appearing on programmes like Blue Peter. When he died in October 1984, the president of the Weimeraner Club of Great Britain was reported in *Dog World* as saying he 'must surely have been the most famous Weimeraner to date'.

Prangen, another Weimeraner, took Thor's place, winning five Kennel Club trials outright and gaining the qualifications of 'companion dog excellent', 'utility dog excellent' and 'working dog excellent'. In addition to normal working-dog duties, Prangen was trained in human remains detection and succeeded in locating a body hidden beneath the foundations of a garden wall.

By the time Prangen retired – he now lives happily in Paul's home – the Metropolitan Police Force were breeding most of their own German Shepherds and Paul was given a puppy called Metpol Dicks. Affectionately, he is called Hobson. As Paul says, he really wanted a Weimeraner and it was Hobson's choice! Hobson quickly won Paul over with his natural abilities as a police dog. They won a place in the central demonstration team and appeared in the centre ring at Crufts in February 1987. They continue working together.

Paul, who is also a judge for Kennel Club Police Dog Championship trials, is totally dedicated to his work. In his spare time he helps friends with their dogs and has trained everything from a Cavalier to a Great Dane.

Lesley Bygrave

Lesley Bygrave is a writer who owns and runs two medical communications companies. She is a lifelong dog owner and lover who believes that owners of badly behaved dogs give the anti-dog lobby just cause for complaint. Up to 1985 she had owned and trained many medium-sized breeds.

In 1985 her world changed with the arrival of Amy Dane, who she says was 'a puppy so big, strong, stubborn and destructive that she was almost indescribable'. Earlier methods used to train smaller breeds did not work on Amy who quickly discovered she was stronger and more stubborn than her owner. A friend introduced Lesley to Paul who, in two hours, had Amy walking at heel and sitting. Lesley still has Amy, who is now a well-behaved four-year-old, 'still stubborn as hell but obedient for me because she's well trained and accepts me as pack leader'.

Troy, a blue Dane, joined them recently and is in training. Troy was taken by the police from cruel owners who chained and starved him. He's about two years old and the opposite to Amy – lovable, nervous and longing to please – so his training is slow and gentle and he is responding well.

Acknowledgements

The authors would like to thank:

- **Margaret Dodd** for supporting her husband and cheerfully putting up with a succession of dogs.
- **The Metropolitan Police** for allowing an active member of the force to collaborate in this book.
- **Malcolm James** for loaning his Doberman, **Jaeger**.
- **John** and **Maureen Pearcy** for loaning **Bruno,** the Rottweiler.
- **Diana Bygrave** for providing help and food at odd times.
- **Kay Keohane** for her housekeeping duties that released writing time.
- Most of all, **Amy Dane**, for being the reason the book was written.

Index

Page numbers in *italics* denote illustrations

Index

THE GERMAN SHEPHERD DOG
Brian H. Wootton
The first truly international book about the world's most popular breed

This important study of the German Shepherd will extend the understanding of both the new owner and the established enthusiast. Drawing upon fascinating sources from Germany, the author traces the development of the breed from its homeland to the various English speaking countries via the most influential bloodlines, including full lists of post-war champions, Grand Victors and Siegers etc.

There is detailed practical information on breeding, rearing puppies and exhibiting; plus a complete chapter on temperament assessment and training, which echoes the author's commitment to the German Shepherd as a working dog. The breed standard is fully discussed and there is invaluable advice on understanding the complex pedigree of imported stud dogs.

The useful appendices include a complete translation of German working trials regulations and glossary of terms.

Lavishly illustrated with photographs (many in colour and unpublished previously), this is the essential book for all German Shepherd lovers.

The Author

Brian Wootton has been actively involved with the German Shepherd dog as breeder, exhibitor, trainer and judge for over 30 years. He has judged in Australia, New Zealand, Africa and the West Indies, as well as at Crufts and other premier breed shows in Britain. He was the first British judge to become a fully accredited S.V. judge, passed by the parent club in Germany. He has always emphasised the dual role of the German Shepherd as both show and working dog, and regularly lectures on the breed at judges' seminars.

THE ROTTWEILER
Jim Pettengell

Few breeds can boast the Rottweiler's recent dramatic rise in numbers. From virtual obscurity in the Fifties, the breed established itself in the Sixties, and then in the Seventies the breed's devotees increased at an alarming rate.

Today, throughout the world, the Rottweiler is rapidly supplanting the Dobermann as the alternative choice to the German Shepherd in the guard dog stakes. This is not without its problems, as the demand for puppies is out-stripping the ability of good breeders to produce quality stock; with the obvious risk of breeding inferior stock. One of the aims of this book is to reduce that risk.

The Rottweiler has been in preparation since 1979 and the result is the most detailed and authoritative work ever published on the breed. As such, it will be in demand by breeders, owners, judges and all students of the Rottweiler.

The text is truly of international appeal, as it researches not only the early history of the breed in Germany but also its progress in most other countries where the Rottweiler has established populations. The work details bloodlines and points out which have proved of value in the various countries.

The character of the breed is another vital area to such a powerful dog and the subject is discussed in great detail as an aid to breeding.

The standard of the breed in Britain, the USA and, most important, in Germany is the subject of much scrutiny. The author's interpretations of the standard, helped by excellent drawings, will be of considerable interest to beginners and experts alike.

The practical aspects of rearing, feeding, breeding, old age and ailments are given careful thought, and the authors' vast experience of the breed (as a show dog and working farm dog) is evident throughout.

The book is full of interesting and valuable photographic

studies of the breed from its establishment through to the present day. Many have never been published before. The appendices contain much supplementary data on clubs, pedigrees, bibliography, translation of German pedigree terms and much more.

The Author

To describe Jim Pettengell as an expert on the breed is an understatement. He ranks as one of the truly pre-eminent authorities. Much of his time is spent travelling the world in order to attend Rottweiler shows and conventions and he is known to anyone who has any knowledge of the breed. His articles are much sought after by breed clubs throughout the world. His own 'Auslese' prefix is synonymous with high quality stock and his champions are eagerly sought for breeding to and from. Unlike many breeders the author expects his stock to prove their ability to herd and work both sheep and cattle in order that these vital qualities are retained within his breeding programme.